teach yourself®

# how to win at horse racing

belinda levez



For over 60 years, more than 40 million people have learnt over 750 subjects the **teach yourself** way, with impressive results.

be where you want to be
with **teach yourself**

For UK orders: please contact Bookpoint Ltd., 130 Milton Park, Abingdon, Oxon OX14 4SB. Telephone: +44 (0)1235 827720. Fax: +44 (0)1235 400454. Lines are open from 09.00–18.00, Monday to Saturday, with a 24-hour message answering service. You can also order through our website www.madaboutbooks.co.uk.

For USA order enquiries: please contact McGraw-Hill Customer Services, PO Box 545, Blacklick, OH 43004-0545, USA. Telephone: 1-800-722-4726. Fax: 1-614-755-5645.

For Canada order enquiries: please contact McGraw-Hill Ryerson Ltd., 300 Water St, Whitby, Ontario L1N 9B6, Canada. Telephone: 905 430 5000. Fax: 905 430 5020.

Long renowned as the authoritative source for self-guided learning – with more than 30 million copies sold worldwide – the *Teach Yourself* series includes over 300 titles in the fields of languages, crafts, hobbies, business, computing and education.

*British Library Cataloguing in Publication Data*
A catalogue record for this title is available from
The British Library

*Library of Congress Catalog Card Number:* On file

First published in UK 1996 by Hodder Headline Plc., 338 Euston Road, London, NW1 3BH.

First published in US 1996 by Contemporary Books, A Division of The McGraw-Hill Companies, 1 Prudential Plaza, 130 East Randolph Street, Chicago, Illinois 60601 USA.



Typeset by SX Composing DTP, Rayleigh, Essex

Printed in Great Britain for Hodder & Stoughton Educational, a division of Hodder Headline Plc, 338 Euston Road, London NW1 3BH by Cox & Wyman Ltd., Reading, Berkshire.

| | |
|---|---|
| Impression number | 10 9 8 7 6 5 4 3 2 |
| Year | 2007 2006 2005 2004 2003 |

teach yourself®

# how to win at horse racing

# contents

# 1 introduction

You may already be betting on horse racing or have decided that you would like to have a bet. Many people gamble on horse racing with varying degrees of success. Some win money but many lose. Some of the losses could be avoided as they are often incurred owing to a lack of knowledge about horse racing and betting. Too many people rely on luck instead of skill.

*How to Win at Horse Racing* is a course of self-study that will help you to identify the factors you need to consider when gambling on horse racing. It will help you to make better decisions based on the way that the industry works.

This book aims to teach you how to get better value. When you are gambling on horse racing you need to overcome the bookmaker's advantage. You will be shown how profitable the various bets are so that you can make an informed choice about those that are worth playing. You are also taught how to obtain the best price.

You are made aware of the ways that bookmakers try to entice you to spend more money. Advice is given on where to gamble. The dangers involved with betting illegally are highlighted.

By the end of the course you will be a more informed gambler with a better understanding of the subject and, hopefully, a winner instead of a loser. Good luck!

# 01 horse racing

**In this chapter you will learn:**

- about the history of horse racing
- about the organization of horse racing
- about racing around the world.

# Origins of horse racing

Horse racing is a sport where two or more specially bred horses are raced around a track, across a predetermined distance, for a prize. It has existed for thousands of years, virtually since horses were first tamed and ridden. Chariot racing, the forerunner of harness racing, was probably the earliest form of the sport and was particularly popular in Ancient Greece and Rome. The first recorded mounted races were run in Ancient Greece.

Modern horse racing originated in England during the twelfth century with the importation of Arab stallions. These horses, valued for their speed and stamina, were bred with English mares to produce racehorses. For the aristocracy, racing horses was a popular pastime. Early races were matches (two horse races) for private bets. The competitors would race across country. Often church towers would be used as landmarks to denote the start and finish of a race. This led to the term 'steeplechase', which is still used today for jump races. In 1174, the Smithfield Track opened in London. Races were also held at fairs across the country.

Horse racing is known as the sport of kings. This title dates back to the time of King Charles II and stems from his interest in breeding and racing horses. This royal connection with horse racing continues today with Queen Elizabeth II who has a keen interest in the breeding and racing of horses.

During the 1700s racecourses opened all over England and transformed horse racing into a professional sport. In 1750 an organization called the Jockey Club was formed to control and administer English racing. The Jockey Club laid down the rules of racing and classified the races. In 1814 five races considered to be the most challenging were designated the classics and survive to the present day. These are the Derby, the Oaks, the 1000 Guineas, the 2000 Guineas and the St Leger. Gradually the value of the purses (prizes) increased, making the racing and breeding of horses a profitable pastime.

Horse racing was introduced to America when the country was first settled. English immigrants brought thoroughbred horses with them and, in 1665, a racetrack was established on Long Island. In common with England, races were designated as classics. Horse racing rose in popularity and by 1890 there were 314 racetracks. However, corruption was rife. To combat this the American Jockey Club was formed in 1894. It was moulded on the English Jockey Club and laid down rules to ensure that horse racing was fair. However, a ban on bookmaking resulted in the decline of horse racing and by 1908 only 25 tracks survived. The introduction of pari-mutuel betting for the Kentucky Derby in 1908 led to a revival. In return for a share of the profits from betting, more and more states legalized pari-mutuel betting. This system continues today.

## Thoroughbred horses

The Jockey Club allocated James Weatherby the task of tracing the pedigree of every racehorse in England. In 1791 he published the *Introduction to the General Stud Book*. To the present day, details of every thoroughbred foal born in England are recorded in the *General Stud Book*. By the early 1800s only horses listed in the *General Stud Book* were allowed to race. As horse racing developed around the world, other countries began their own stud books. The *American Stud Book*, recording the pedigree of all thoroughbred racehorses foaled, was started in 1868.

Horses listed in the *General Stud Book* are called thoroughbreds. A thoroughbred is a horse descended from one of three stallions, the Darley Arabian (1724), the Godolphin Arabian (1724) and the Byerley Turk (1680). Thoroughbred horses compete in flat and national hunt/steeplechase racing. The date of birth of thoroughbreds is the 1 January, regardless of when they were actually born. They begin their training as yearlings when they learn to accept a saddle, bridle and rider. They are then trained to go into the starting stalls and run around a track. They usually begin their racing careers as 2-year-olds. Although their peak racing age is 5 years, those with excellent winning records are often retired earlier to go to stud.

## Types of racing

### Flat racing

Flat racing refers to the fact that no jumping is involved. The actual racecourses are rarely flat as many tracks have uphill or downhill slopes. The races tend to be short with many sprints. The length of the races varies from short sprints of around 5 furlongs (1005 metres) to longer races of around 2 miles (3.2 km). In the USA races tend to be shorter and are between 5 and 12 furlongs.

Races take place on a variety of surfaces including turf, dirt, sand and fibre-sand, which is a man-made material.

Starting stalls are used to start flat races to ensure a fair outcome. The starting stalls are operated by a mechanical device and ensure all the horses start the race at the same time. Each compartment of the stalls has doors at the front and the back. The horses are loaded into the back and the doors are closed behind them. When all the horses are loaded, the doors at the front open simultaneously at the off. A draw takes place to determine which stall each runner starts from.

## National hunt races or steeplechases

National hunt races or steeplechases are particularly popular in Great Britain, Ireland and France. This type of racing originated from fox hunting. The races are held over obstacles like brush fences, wooden rails, stone walls and water-filled ditches. The obstacles vary in size from hurdles of around 1 to 2 feet (30–60 cm) to the enormous Grand National fences. Jumpers generally compete over hurdles before graduating to the larger obstacles. Hurdle races are for horses aged 3 years after 1 July. National hunt races are run over longer distances than flat races and are usually started with a starting gate or by flag. The hurdle races start from 2 miles. Steeplechases can be as long as 4½ miles.

The horses taking part in steeplechases tend to be bigger and older than those competing in flat racing. They are specially bred to give a combination of size, speed and stamina. The horses start racing from the age of 4 years after 1 July. It is not unusual for the horses to continue racing until they are 10 years or older. Red Rum, for example, was 12 years old when he won the Grand National for the third time.

There are also some races for national hunt horses, which have no obstacles. They are called national hunt flat races and are run across national hunt courses. These races are for horses aged between 4 and 6 years that have not raced in any other official races.

## Harness racing

Modern harness racing originated in the USA during the eighteenth century when it was a popular pastime for individuals to race each other over country roads. The country's fairs became a major venue for organized races. The first racetracks were established at the beginning of the nineteenth century. In 1939 the United States Trotting Association was established. It is responsible for the registration of standardbreds (the horses) and keeping records of each horse's racing career. After 1900 harness racing declined, mainly due to the introduction of the automobile. In 1940, Roosevelt Raceway in New York introduced floodlit harness racing with pari-mutuel betting, which boosted the popularity of the sport. Nowadays, harness racing is found all over the USA and is particularly popular in the Midwest and East. Harness racing is also found in continental Europe, Canada, Australia and New Zealand.

Harness racing is run on an oval-shaped dirt track. Most races are 1 mile long and are usually run anti-clockwise. The jockey, called a driver, sits in the harness, called a sulky or racebike. The horses must trot and are disqualified if they break into a gallop for too long. If a horse breaks into a gallop, the driver must bring the horse back to its correct gait and lose ground to the other competitors.

## Standardbred horses

Standardbred horses compete in harness racing. They are smaller than thoroughbreds and more muscular, with a long body and bigger head. Standardbred horses originated in the 1780s from an English thoroughbred, Messenger, which was exported to the USA. One of its descendants was Hambletonian 10, from which all standardbred horses are descended. These horses are so called because the early trotters had to reach a certain standard over the mile distance to gain registration as a standardbred. They start racing as 2- or 3-year-olds.

There are two types of standardbred – trotters and pacers. The difference between them is in the way they move. Pacers are faster than trotters and make up around 80 per cent of harness racers. Often called sidewheelers, they move with the legs on one side of their body in unison (front right and back right together, and front left and back left together). Pacers are fitted with plastic loops called hobbles, which are an aid to maintaining the correct gait. If a horse runs without hobbles it is called free-legged. Trotters move with a diagonal gait (front right and back left together, and front left and back right together).

Trotting races are usually started from a standing position. Pacing races are generally started with a moving start. A starting gate is attached to a vehicle. When the judge is satisfied that the horses are all level with the gate, the vehicle accelerates away.

## Grading of races

There is a hierarchy of races. The more prestigious a race, the higher its purse. In Great Britain, flat races are graded into groups and classes. The races are classified from A to G inclusive, where A is the highest and G the lowest. Class A is subdivided into three levels of group races. Group 1 races are the highest and group 3 the lowest.

The rating of the horse determines which group or class it races in. Its rating is calculated by a team of six handicappers appointed by the British Horse Racing Board. They assess the performance of each horse by watching races live and viewing the steward's tapes of the races. They give each horse a rating on a scale of 0 to 140, the latter being the highest. The top horses are those with a rating over 110 and they compete in the best races.

The national hunt races are divided into grades as follows:

- Grade 1, 2, 3
- Grade 1 Novice
- Grade 2 Novice
- Grade 1 NHF (national hunt flat)
- Grade 2 NHF
- Grades B to H inclusive.

In the USA the stakes races are divided into groups. Group numbers are denoted by roman numerals. Group I races are the highest and group III the lowest. In harness racing they are grouped as A, B and C, with group A races the highest and group C the lowest. Other races are ungraded which include claiming races where the horses competing in the race may be purchased by registered owners at a set price. Ownership of the horse changes as soon as the race is off. Allowance races are for apprentice jockeys where the jockeys are allowed to claim a weight allowance.

## Handicaps

A handicap is a race where the chances of all the competitors winning are evened out by handicapping them with extra weight. If the handicapper does his or her job correctly then all the horses should cross the line at the same time. The horses that are deemed to have the best chance of winning are required to carry the greatest amount of weight. The weight is added by means of lead bars that are inserted into the saddle. The jockeys are weighed with their saddles both before and after the race to ensure that they are carrying the correct weight. Occasionally these weights can fall off in the course of the race. This leads to disqualification of the horse.

## Conditional races

For many races there are conditions placed on entry. There may be age restrictions, for example races for 2-year-old or 3-year-old horses. Others may be for apprentice jockeys or women jockeys or amateur riders. Races may be for maidens – horses that have never won before. In Great Britain there are selling races, where the winner is auctioned after the race.

## Gambling on horse racing

Gambling on horse racing started virtually as soon as horse racing was invented. The matches would often be subject to a private wager or 'gentlemen's agreement'. With the organization of racecourses, came bookmakers who would act as a banker and agree to cover everyone's bets. However, their actions were often far from gentlemanly and they were notorious for welshing on bets. This led to many countries either outlawing bookmakers or introducing legislation, which governed the way in which they could operate. Some countries also introduced state-operated betting to ensure that bettors would get a fair deal.

### Why bet on horse racing?

Many forms of gambling rely on pure luck. Horse racing differs. It is possible for a gambler to assess the runners in a race and to use his or her skill and judgement to predict the winner.

There are many issues that you need to consider before you bet. You may already know some gamblers; they have probably recounted stories of their big wins. However, it is highly unlikely that they have told you how much money they have lost. A lot of gamblers will tell you that they always break even; if this is true, why do bookmakers make such huge profits? No matter what other gamblers tell you, do not assume that it is easy to win.

Gambling is risky. You can easily lose. No matter how well you have assessed the runners, there are always unpredictable things that can happen. Your horse may be brought down by a loose horse, or the jockey could inadvertently take the wrong course, which would lead to disqualification.

When gamblers start losing there is a tendency to try to recoup losses by betting more heavily. This can lead to financial ruin. Gambling can also become addictive, if you find that your betting is getting out of control, you should contact one of the Gamblers Anonymous organizations. Details are given on page 105. You can guard against this situation arising by ensuring that you take a sensible approach to gambling.

## How fair is betting?

In many countries betting operations are state controlled to safeguard the public against unscrupulous operators. Most countries have introduced some form of gambling legislation to set out the conditions under which betting on horse racing is allowed.

In the UK the relevant legislation is the Betting, Gaming and Lotteries Act 1963. Bookmakers are required to be licensed by the Betting Licensing Committee at the local Magistrates Court. In order to gain a permit a bookmaker must show that he or she is a fit and proper person. Regulations also determine when and how a bookmaker can operate his or her business.

There is currently a great deal of concern over the fairness of web sites offering online betting services. Internet betting has caused a number of problems as web sites are often run by offshore companies. This makes them difficult to prosecute if they break an individual country's laws on gambling. The Australian government has gone some way to addressing this problem by introducing a system of licensing for web sites offering gambling services. However, this does not completely safeguard punters against unscrupulous operators as web sites have been set up which appear to be based in Australia but are in fact offshore businesses. If you intend to bet over the internet it pays to be extremely cautious.

In the both the US and Great Britain, gambling debts are not recoverable at law. In Great Britain an organization has been set up to resolve punters' disputes with bookmakers. The Independent Betting Arbitration Service (IBAS) was established in 1998. It offers a free arbitration service to customers of bookmakers who are registered with the IBAS. Bookmakers in the scheme have agreed to co-operate with any investigations into their operations and to abide by decisions made by the IBAS. If a bookmaker fails to abide by the scheme, he or she may have renewal of his or her betting permit refused.

## How fair is racing?

The various controlling bodies of racing go to great lengths to ensure that racing is fair. For example, in Great Britain where the Jockey Club administers horse racing there are strict controls in place. The Jockey Club is actively involved in detecting any form of foul play by gathering intelligence, carrying out surveillance and monitoring moves in the betting market. If they suspect foul play, they investigate the matter and pass their findings on to police. The Jockey Club is also responsible for racecourse security and uses closed-circuit television (CCTV) at racecourse stables. The Jockey Club also appoints stewards who ensure that the rules of racing are followed. At each race meeting the stewards watch the races live. They also have access to all the tape recordings of races made at vantage points around the course. If there is an infringement of the rules they have the power to amend the result, disqualify runners or void a race.

Britain bans the use of performance-enhancing drugs in horse racing. Programmes are in place to test horses for doping. Each year around 10 per cent of horses are dope tested. The incidence of horses being tested positive is extremely low.

In the past, race fixers would substitute a horse for a ringer (a horse of similar appearance that has a greater chance of winning). This has been combated by issuing all thoroughbred racehorses, registered in the *General Stud Book*, with passports at birth. This document includes details of their pedigree, colour and distinguishing markings. Random checks are carried out at racecourses to verify the identity of horses. In addition blood samples can be taken and analysed and compared to those taken from the horse on registration. From 1 January 1999, thoroughbreds were microchipped. A microchip inserted into the horse's neck can be scanned to confirm the horse's identity.

# A day at the races

Spending a day at the races is one of the most enjoyable aspects of betting on horse racing. You have the thrill of watching the race at close quarters as the horses thunder along the rails, and are directly involved in the hustle and bustle of the betting ring as bets are laid.

Horse races are arranged into meetings with a programme of racing that will fill either a morning, afternoon or evening. Races are generally timed to take place at roughly 30-minute intervals.

## Planning your day

Information about forthcoming meetings is advertised in the racing newspapers. For most meetings it is not necessary to book tickets, you simply pay on arrival at the course. If you plan to attend a major race day, it is best to book tickets in advance, particularly for the more expensive areas of the course. Also check the dress code. On some race days members are required to wear morning dress and women are asked to wear hats. For most other race days smart dress of jacket and tie for men is a necessary requirement in the members area. Make sure you are wearing comfortable shoes, as you are likely to do a lot of walking.

Before you start your journey to a race meeting always check that the racing is still going ahead, particularly if the weather is bad. Frost, snow, heavy fog or waterlogged tracks can all be reasons for a meeting being abandoned. You can find up-to-date information on the internet, teletext services, radio and television broadcasts.

Allow plenty of time for your journey and bear in mind that there may be heavy traffic near the racecourse. If you are using public transport you will often find that extra buses are laid on. Aim to arrive at least an hour before the first race starts. This will give you enough time to find your way around all the facilities.

Racecourses are divided into different areas, which are priced according to the facilities offered. They are the silver ring, tattersalls and the members' enclosure. Tattersalls usually referred to as tatts is the main area, which includes the grandstand, paddock and winners enclosure. The members' enclosure is the most expensive and gives the best view of the course, particularly of the winning post. You will be issued with a badge, which you should wear to gain access to all the facilities. Spectators in the members' enclosure also gain access to tattersalls. The silver ring is the cheapest area. It is so called because it used to cost less than £1 for admission. Each area of the racecourse will have a range of catering facilities including restaurants, bars and fast-food outlets.

The grandstand provides seating for spectators and gives a good view of the racecourse. Giant television screens give further coverage of the races. During the course of the race, a commentary is given via loudspeakers. The paddock is where the horses are paraded before racing. Here the owners give last-minute instructions to the jockeys before they mount their horses and ride down to the start of the race. For major races the horses are often paraded on the racecourse in front of the grandstand. The winners' enclosure is where the winning and placed horses are displayed at the end of the race. Here a podium is used for presenting prizes.

## The running of a race

The clerk of the course is the person responsible for the running of the racecourse. Before the race, he or she will inspect the course and declare the official going.

Before the start of the race, betting commences with both the bookmakers and the tote. The bookmakers mark their tissue prices on their boards and the tote screens begin to display the approximate odds.

The weighing room is where the jockeys are weighed both before and after the race to ensure that their weight has not changed. The jockeys are all weighed and proceed to the parade ring where they rendezvous with the owners and trainers. The jockeys receive last-minute instructions about how they should run the race. The horses are led to the parade ring by stable staff and are saddled. Around 5 minutes before the off, the jockeys mount the horses and ride down to the start. The announcer will say 'they're going down'.

The starter will indicate that he is ready to start the race often by raising a flag. The announcer will say 'they're under orders'.

When the starter is satisfied that the horses are ready to start the race, it will be declared off. The announcer will say 'they're off'. As soon as the race is off, betting stops. This will often be accompanied by a ringing bell to indicate that betting has stopped. With long national hunt races, some bookmakers may continue to accept bets for a short while after the off or until a horse falls. Occasionally there will be a false start and the horses will be recalled.

Commentary will be given about the race. A number of Jockey Club officials called 'stewards' watch each race to ensure that they are fairly run. The race is also recorded via a number of cameras set at different vantage points.

The finish of each race is photographed and if the race is particularly close, the film will be developed and scrutinized to determine the winner. The race result will be announced. The winning and placed horses are ridden to the winners' enclosure. The jockeys then proceed to the weighing room to weigh in. If the stewards are satisfied that the race was fairly run, the announcement 'weighed in' will be given. Winning bets are then paid out. If a steward's enquiry or objection is announced, there will be a delay in giving the 'weighed in' announcement and in paying out the winning bets until the incident leading to the enquiry or objection has been fully investigated. After the investigation an announcement 'result stands', 'amended result' or 'race void' will be given. 'Result stands' means that the stewards are satisfied that the race was fairly run. 'Amended result' means that the stewards have decided that the rules of racing have been broken. They may disqualify a competitor or declare a different winner or placed horses. If the race is declared void, stakes will be refunded to the punters. Later, a short ceremony is held to present the prizes and trophies won for the race.

## Identifying the runners

Each horse has a number marked on its saddlecloth that corresponds to its number on the race card. The vast majority of racehorses are varying shades of brown, which makes them difficult to identify at a distance. To help spectators identify their horses, the jockeys wear silks, which are brightly coloured shirts, and cap covers. Owners have their own colours, which are registered. Details of the colours worn by each jockey are given on the race card. Binoculars are useful for watching the runners at a distance. If you do not have your own, it is possible to hire them at the racecourse for a small fee.

## Owning a racehorse

An added thrill to betting on horse racing is owning your own horse. Nowadays you do not have to be wealthy to own a racehorse. It is possible to buy a share in a horse through partnerships and clubs. Costs vary from between US $3,500–50,000 per share. Details of partnerships and clubs are advertised in horse racing media.

Due to the high prize money paid, Hong Kong is one of the most profitable places to run a horse. Purses are equivalent to around four times those paid in the UK. Around 47 per cent of the horses in Hong Kong earn enough to cover their costs. A successful horse can be highly profitable. Owners invested HK $325,000 in a horse called Quicken Away and won HK $8.75 million (US $1.1 million) in prizes.

## Racing around the world

### Great Britain

The British Horse Racing Board governs racing in Great Britain. There are 59 racecourses, which are all different. Most races take place on turf. Three racecourses have fibre-sand tracks, which allow racing to go ahead in adverse weather conditions. These are Lingfield Park, Southwell and Wolverhampton. On average there are three to four race meetings taking place daily. Flat racing dominates in spring and summer, with national hunt racing during autumn and winter. There is no harness racing except for a few novelty events. Racing takes place all year round with the exception of Christmas Day and Good Friday.

Britain has legal independent on-course bookmakers and tote betting. There are also on-course betting shops where it is also possible to bet on races at other meetings. In addition there are 8500 off-course betting shops which show live racing via satellite on television screens. The off-course shops take bets on the average odds offered by the on-course bookmakers, tote bets and they offer telephone betting facilities in the form of deposit and credit accounts. On-course betting with bookmakers is tax-free. Off-course betting was abolished in 2001.

### The main events of the racing calendar

The most important races are the classics for 3-year olds – 2000 Guineas, 1000 Guineas, the Derby, Oaks and St Leger. The 2000 Guineas and 1000 Guineas are run over the Rowley Mile Course at Newmarket in May. The Derby and the Oaks are staged at Epsom Downs. The Derby, which was first run in 1780, attracts the best horses from around the world. It is a 1½ mile race for 3-year-old colts and has over £1 million in prize money. The Oaks is the Derby's counterpart for fillies. The St Leger is the world's oldest classic and is held at Doncaster in September. A horse that wins the 2000 Guineas, Derby and St Leger in the same year gains the Triple Crown title.

Other major flat races include the Gold Cup and the Spring Double. The Gold Cup, a race over 2½ miles is the premier race of the Royal Ascot meeting. First held in 1807, it is run on the third day of the meeting. The Spring Double is the name given to the Lincolnshire and the Grand National. The Autumn Double is the Cesarewitch and the Cambridgeshire. The Cesarewitch is a handicap race held in late October at Newmarket. The race dates from 1839 and was named to honour the state visit of Russian prince, Alexander II (*tsesarevich* means 'heir to the throne').

The most famous national hunt race is the Grand National, which is a steeplechase handicap run at Aintree, England, in April. The race, first run in 1839, is a true test of endurance with the horses competing over a distance of 4 miles and 856 yards. Just completing the course without falling is a huge challenge. In 1928, only two horses managed to finish. There are 30 fences to be jumped which are notoriously difficult, especially Beecher's Brook and Valentine's Brook which are water jumps. The Grand National holds the record for the most runners in a race – in 1929, 66 horses competed.

Other major national hunt races include the Cheltenham Festival and the King George VI & Queen Elizabeth Diamond Stakes. The Cheltenham Festival is the premier national hunt meeting and is held in March. It features the Champion Hurdle and the Cheltenham Gold Cup. Kempton Park hosts the King George VI & Queen Elizabeth Diamond Stakes on Boxing Day (26 December).

## Ireland

The Irish Turf Club, established in 1790, controls racing in Ireland. A new body created in 1994, the Irish Horse Racing

Authority, is responsible for administering government grants to the industry. Ireland has a thriving stud-farm industry and is world renowned for the breeding of horses.

There are 27 major racecourses. All are turf except for Laytown where races are run on the sandy beach. A mixture of flat and jump meetings are held. Racing takes place seven days a week, including Sundays.

There is on-course betting with bookmakers, which is tax-free, as well as tote betting. There are also 900 off-course betting shops with betting on both Irish and British racing which is televised via satellite. Off-course bets are taxed at 5 per cent.

The Curragh is the headquarters of flat racing, staging all five classic races – the Irish Derby, the Irish 1000 and 2000 Guineas, the Irish Oaks and the Irish St Leger.

Leopardstown is the major national hunt venue. It also hosts flat meetings and in September it stages the Champion Stakes, which is a World Series of Racing event. The course is also host to the Irish Gold Cup in February.

Ireland has five major festivals of racing – Galway, Listowel, Tralee, Killarney and the Derby Festival at the Curragh. At the festival meetings racing takes place for between three and seven days. Galway is the most famous, lasting for seven days. In addition to the racing there are many other entertainment activities, including live music, exhibitions, fairs and competitions.

## The USA

In the USA racing is controlled by state racing commissions. They are responsible for the issuing of licences and approving racing fixtures. Together with the Jockey Club they appoint racing officials and ensure racing rules are adhered to. Racing takes place all year round. Meetings often last for over ten weeks. There are over 500 racetracks, which vary little – all tend to be oval-shaped dirt tracks with left-hand bends. The emphasis is on speed, with lots of short races. The US Trotting Association promotes harness racing, which is more popular than thoroughbred racing, with more tracks and more races each year. National hunt racing is only found at a few meetings. It is regulated by the National Steeplechase and Hunt Association.

On-course betting is via the pari-mutuel system, although it is estimated that betting with illegal bookmakers far exceeds betting on the tote. In some states there is legal off-course betting. These states include Arizona, Connecticut, Illinois, Louisiana, Nebraska, Nevada, New York, North Dakota, Oregon, Pennsylvania, Washington State and Wyoming.

### The main events of the racing calendar

The US classics are the Belmont Stakes, the Preakness Stakes and the Kentucky Derby. Each race makes up one leg of the Triple Crown. The Kentucky Derby, first run in 1875, is held at Churchill Downs near Louisville, Kentucky. It is run over 1¼ miles on the first Saturday of May. This race forms the first leg of the Triple Crown. The Preakness Stakes dates from 1873. It is held at Pimlico and is run over 1³⁄₁₆ miles. The Belmont Stakes was first run in 1867. Throughout its history the race was run over various distances. It is now run over 1½ miles and it takes place five weeks after the Kentucky Derby at Belmont Park in Elmont New York.

Other major races include The Breeders' Cup Classic and Turf and the Arlington Million. These races form part of the World Series of Racing. The Breeders' Cup races are held at Churchill Downs in Louisville, Kentucky, during late October or early November. The Breeders' Cup Turf is run over 1½ miles with a US $2 million prize. The Breeders' Cup Classic is over 1¼ miles for a prize of US $4 million. The Arlington Million, which is held at Arlington Park in Chicago, was the first race to offer a US $1 million prize. The race over 1¼ miles on turf is now worth US $2 million.

The Breeders' Cup Steeplechase is held at Far Hills, New Jersey. Horses of 4 years and up compete over 2⅝ miles for the country's largest steeplechase prize. Three of the country's oldest steeplechase races are still run today – the Maryland Cup (1894), the American Grand National (1899) and the National Hunt Cup (1909).

In harness racing the richest race is the Hambletonian. The race for 3-year-olds is held at Meadowlands Racetrack in East Rutherford, New Jersey. It has a purse of over US $1 million. The race takes is name from the stallion, Hambletonian, which was born in Orange County, New York, on 5 May 1849. As a 3-year-old it trotted a mile in 2 minutes 48½ seconds. It was put to stud and sired 1331 foals, including Dexter, which became a world champion trotter in 1867. The Hambletonian, Yonkers Trot and the Kentucky Futurity make up the trotting Triple

Crown. The pacers Triple Crown is the Little Brown Jug, the Messenger Stakes and the Cane Pace.

## Continental Europe

There is horse racing across most of continental Europe, dominated by harness racing. In Eastern Europe, the Netherlands and Belgium, the introduction of satellite technology has resulted in a large amount of betting taking place on foreign racing (mostly British and Irish). In Eastern Europe betting is via casinos and cafés on the tote. Belgium has on-course bookmakers, tote and off-course betting shops. Italy has off-course betting shops, which allow betting on the tote. In Scandinavian countries, betting is via the tote. European operators have also innovated a system of commingling tote pools which creates potentially bigger payouts

### France

France has a state-run horse racing industry controlled by the National Federation of French Racing. There are 260 race-courses with a mixture of flat, steeplechase and harness racing. Bookmakers are illegal so betting is on the state-run tote (the PMU, or pari-mutuel). Bets may be placed on course or in betting shops and cafés. A recent change has been the innovation of off-course race-by-race betting. The trifecta and superfecta bets are particularly popular.

The French classics are the Prix du Jockey Club (1836), the Grand Prix du Paris (1863) and the Prix de l'Arc de Triomphe (1920). Longchamp just outside Paris, plays host to the Prix de L'Arc de Triomphe which is Europe's richest race with a prize of FF 10.5 million (roughly US $1.5 million).

## Australia

In Australia there is racing all year round. Australia has 380 racecourses that are mostly turf. There is a mixture of racing including flat racing, which is called 'gallops' and steeplechase races. Harness racing is particularly popular and is generally referred to as 'the trots'. There are 206 clubs that organize races.

Betting is with on-course bookmakers and tote betting. Tote bets can also be placed at off-course betting shops, pubs, casinos and over the telephone. Popular bets are the quinella (reversed forecast) place and the tierce or trifecta (tricast). The quinella place is selecting any two of the first three placed horses in any order.

The Melbourne Cup is a race that dates from 1861. Traditionally it is held on the first Tuesday in November at the Flemington Race Course. It is Australia's richest race with a purse of AUS $3 million (roughly US $2 million). The Cox Plate is held in October at Moonee Valley, Melbourne. Runners compete on turf, over 2040 metres, for a prize of AUS $1 million. The Miracle Mile is Australia's richest pacing race.

## New Zealand

Horse racing in New Zealand is governed by the Racing Industry Board and operated by individual clubs. There are 155 clubs that organize race meetings at 71 racetracks. There is thoroughbred racing on turf and harness racing on mostly all-weather surfaces (around 10 per cent of harness racing is on turf). Betting is controlled by the TAB and is available both on and off course on either the tote or fixed odds. There are 510 off-course betting outlets run by the TAB. The TAB also operates telephone betting services and an internet site.

## South Africa

South Africa has 15 racetracks. The tracks are owned and operated by race clubs. Betting is with the tote, on-course bookmakers and off-course tote outlets. There is also telephone betting.

Major races include the Summer Handicap and the July. The Summer Handicap is the country's richest and is held in November at the Turffontein Racecourse, Johannesburg. Three-year-olds and up compete over 2000 metres for a R1.2 million prize (approximately US $156,000). The July, a race dating from 1897, takes place at Greyville racetrack, Durban. It is run on the first Saturday of July over a distance of 2200 metres for a prize of R1 million (around US $130,500).

## Canada

Horse racing in Canada is governed by the Canadian Pari-Mutuel Association. Each province has a racing commission, which is responsible for ensuring the rules of racing are adhered to. Canada has 40 racetracks offering both thoroughbred and harness racing. Betting is via the pari-mutuel and includes betting on US horse racing. The Canadian International, part of the World Series of Racing, is held at Woodbine Racetrack in October. Three-year-olds and up compete over 1 mile 4 furlongs (1½ miles) for a purse of C $1,500,00 (around US $2 million). Other major races include the Molson Mile, the Queen's Plate, the Western Canada Derby Series and the Gold Cup and Saucer.

## Japan

Japan has 37 racecourses with tote betting, off-course betting outlets and telephone betting facilities. The races are organized by the Japanese Racing Association (JRA) and local government. The top horses (around 6500) are registered with the JRA, which organizes races at ten courses across Japan. The Japan Cup, part of the World Series of Racing, is held at Tokyo Race course in November. Three-year-olds and up compete over 2400 metres (about 1½ miles) on turf for a purse of over US $4.5 million.

## Hong Kong

Hong Kong has two racecourses – Sha Tin and Happy Valley. Happy Valley dates from 1846 and hosts a programme of races from September to June. Sha Tin is the venue for prestigious international events including the Hong Kong Cup, which is part of the World Series and takes place in December. Three-year-olds and up compete over 2000 metres (1¼ miles) for a purse of US $1.8 million.

## The World Series Racing Championship

In common with other sports, it was decided to organize a World Series championship for horse racing. The first event took place in 1999. Horses may compete in races held across four continents. The competition features some of the world's most prestigious races. The first race in the series is the Dubai World Cup run, over 1¼ miles on dirt, at the Nad Al Sheba Racecourse in Dubai, United Arab Emirates. With a prize of US $6 million it is the world's richest race. It was established in 1996 and is viewed in over 197 countries. The other qualifying races are the King George VI & Queen Elizabeth Diamond Stakes, the Arlington Million, the Grosser Preis Von Baden, the Irish Champion Stakes, the Canadian International, the Cox Plate, the Breeders' Cup Classic, Breeders' Cup Turf, Japan Cup and the Hong Kong Cup.

The first six horses in each race are allocated points based on the system used for Formula One Grand Prix as follows:

- first place – 12 points
- second place – 6 points
- third place – 4 points
- fourth place – 3 points
- fifth place – 2 points
- sixth place – 1 point

# 02 where to bet

**In this chapter you will learn:**

- **about the different types of betting**
- **the advantages and disadvantages of each type of betting**
- **about the variety of bets.**

Your choice of where to bet will be limited by where you live. Legislation in some countries outlaws some forms of betting while allowing others. Some countries, such as Great Britain, have liberal gaming laws, which allow betting to take place on and off course, over the telephone and via the internet. In other places betting is only allowed on course.

## On-course bookmakers

Bookmaking is a system of betting on fixed odds or prices. Bookmakers are independent operators who take bets on horse racing. This system of betting exists alongside the tote. Unlike the tote, the money bet does not go into a pool. Instead the customer bets against the individual bookmaker at odds that are agreed at the time the bet is placed. It is much like a bet between two individuals. This means that when you place your bet with a bookmaker, you can immediately calculate how much you could win.

A number of countries including Great Britain, Ireland, Belgium, Australia and South Africa have legal bookmakers. They carry out their business at the racecourse in designated areas. Some countries do not allow bookmaking.

In the silver ring and tattersalls each bookmaker is allocated a pitch or stand. They advertise the prices they are offering on each horse on boards or electronic displays. For each race, the horses names, race card number and odds offered are marked. These bookmakers cater for low-staking punters.

Rails bookmakers are located in a separate area, usually along the rail that separates the members' enclosure from tattersalls. They take bets from high-staking punters, other bookmakers and credit customers. Their prices are not advertised on boards; instead they simply make a note of all bets placed.

The range of bets offered by bookmakers is limited mostly to win and each-way bets. When you have selected a bookmaker, tell him or her your selection, the type of bet you want and your stake. You can either just call out the price on offer or announce the returns to the stakes. Suppose you wanted to bet £8 on Dobbin to win at 6/1. You can simply announce '£8 on Dobbin to win at 6/1'. Alternatively you can say '48 to 8 Dobbin'.

When you place a bet you will be given a ticket with the bookmaker's name and a number on it. The ticket has no details about your selection or how much you have staked. All of those details appear in the bookmaker's ledger. It is therefore important that you listen to make sure that the bookmaker correctly repeats your bet, as the clerk will write down whatever the bookmaker shouts out. If you think a mistake has been made, query it immediately. Pay particular attention if there are two or more horses with similar names in the same race. Also make a note of the bet yourself. If you make several bets you may not remember all the details of each bet.

Be sure to place your bet in good time, as there is always a last-minute rush. If you leave it too late you may not get your bet on. You will only be able to collect your winnings from the bookmaker with whom you placed the bet, as they are all independent.

There are several advantages to betting with bookmakers at the racecourse. In Great Britain and Ireland the bets are tax-free which gives respectively a 9 per cent or 5 per cent saving over betting shops. You get to see the horses in the paddock before they run. This gives you the opportunity to see the horse's condition at close quarters and to spot anything amiss that may affect its running. You get to see the racing live. This means that if you see an incident, which leads to a stewards' enquiry or objection, or are well placed to judge which horse has won a photo finish, you can make some extra money by betting on the outcome. You also have more choice, as the prices that individual bookmakers offer will vary. You have the opportunity to shop around for the best price. A lot of betting takes place before prices are transmitted to betting shops so you are able to take advantage of earlier shows. You also have the chance to negotiate a better price with the bookmaker, as they are all independent. You are able to take a fixed price, and so know exactly what you will win. You can also compare the prices on offer from the bookmakers with those on the tote.

There are some disadvantages too. You have to pay for admission charges and for the cost of travelling. It is also time-consuming to go to a race meeting.

You will need to decide for yourself whether or not it is cost-effective to attend the meeting or whether you should simply go to a betting shop. The deciding factor will most likely be your level of stakes. If you intend to place large bets, you are likely to benefit from attending the meeting. If your bets will be small, any advantages in prices and tax-free betting will tend to be outweighed by the admission and travelling costs.

# Tote betting and pari-mutuel

## Tote betting

Tote is short for totalizator, which is a betting system where the total of the bets on a race are divided among those betting on the winner. A deduction is made for tax, money returned to racing and running costs. The amount deducted varies from country to country.

This system is completely independent of bookmakers and any bets placed with bookmakers do not affect the winnings paid. The prices offered by bookmakers bear no relation to the prices paid on the tote.

At the racecourse you will see a large board showing the number of bets placed on each runner, the total value of the bets and the payouts. Alternatively these details will be displayed on television screens. There are different figures for different types of bets. These figures are constantly changing as more money is bet. As soon as the race is off, betting stops.

If you have bet on a horse to win and it comes in first, you will have a share of the win pool. The amount you win will depend on how many other people also have selected the winner, much like a lottery. If you are the only person who has picked the winner then you will receive all the money in the win pool. If 500 people have bet on the winner then you will receive 1/500 of the pool.

The highest recorded tote odds for a win bet were 3410¼/1. They were paid on a horse called Coole at British racecourse Haydock Park on 30 November 1929.

In Great Britain the most common tote bets are:

- win – the selection to win
- place – the number of places depends on the number of runners
- each-way – a bet on the horse to win and a bet on the horse to be placed
- exacta – predicting the first and second in correct order
- trifecta – predicting which horses will be first, second and third in the correct order
- quadpot – predicting which horses will be placed in the four quadpot races (usually races 3 to 6)
- jackpot – predicting which horses will win in each race of a meeting (usually the first six races)

- placepot – predicting which horses will be placed in each race of a meeting (usually the first six races)
- scoop 6 – selecting the winners in six nominated televized races
- multibets like doubles trebles, accumulator, patent, yankee or super 15 can also be played

Dividends are quoted to a £1 stake.

For place bets the number of places that count are as follows:

| Number of runners | Places |
|---|---|
| 1–4 | Win only |
| 5–7 | First and second |
| 8+ | First, second and third |
| 16+ handicaps | First, second, third and fourth |

## Pari-mutuel

Pari-mutuel is basically a similar system to tote betting with slightly different rules. The money on each selection is also pooled and divided between the winners after deductions. The main difference is the way that horses from the same stable are treated. If, for example, horses A and B are running from the same stable, they are coupled. This means that a bet for horse A to win, is also a bet for horse B to win. If you place a bet on horse A to win, you will also win if horse B wins the race. The coupling only applies to win bets and not to place, show or exotic bets. (Bets other than win, place and show are called exotics.)

Pari-mutuel betting is found in the USA and continental Europe.

In the United States the most common bets are:

- win – the selection to win
- place – the selection must be first or second
- show – the selection must finish first, second or third
- exacta/perfecta – predicting the first and second in the correct order
- trifecta – predicting the first, second and third in the correct order
- daily double – predicting the winners in the first two races of the day

Dividends are quoted to a US $2 stake.

## Placing your bet

At the racecourse, you simply go to the tote or pari-mutuel counter and tell the member of staff the number of the horse you have selected, the type of bet you want and how much you want to stake. For bets that involve more than one race, like placepot and jackpot, you will usually be required to fill in a betting slip. At some racecourses machines have been installed for issuing tickets.

You will be presented with a printed ticket. Always check that it is marked with the correct details. Keep your ticket in a safe place, as you will need it to collect your winnings. Do not throw it away until after the weigh-in is announced. Even if your horse finished last there could still be a steward's enquiry, which could lead to an amended result or even to a race being declared void. If a race is declared void, you will be entitled to claim your stake back. To collect your winnings simply present your ticket at the payout window.

The rules vary depending on where you bet. For some forecast bets the selections must finish in the correct order; for others the order is not important. You should carefully read the rules and make sure you understand them before you bet.

The advantage of betting on the tote is that you can bet for small stakes. It can be more profitable to back outsiders on the tote, as close to the off their odds are not always lengthened by bookmakers.

The main disadvantage with betting on the tote is that you are betting blind, as you do not know in advance what your winnings will be. When you bet with a bookmaker, you can take the price on offer, so therefore you can work out exactly how much you will win. With the tote you get a rough guide of what the dividends will pay. This is constantly changing and is updated as more bets are placed. The dividend may change hugely between when you put your bet on and when the race is declared off. There may be a flurry of betting with the bookmakers, which drastically lowers the price of a horse. This may prompt those betting on the tote also to back this horse, which will drive down the dividend for that particular horse. It is not until after the race that you will know exactly how much the dividends will pay. There is also the disadvantage of the high deduction for costs such as tax.

# Off-course betting

In Great Britain there are licensed betting shops. In recent years there has been much deregulation, which has allowed extended opening hours to cover evening and Sunday racing. They offer a wide range of facilities including:

- betting on virtually any sporting event
- a wide range of different bets
- live transmission of horse racing, greyhound racing and other sporting events
- amusement machines
- refreshments
- telephone betting
- credit and deposit accounts

The pages of the major sporting newspapers are arranged around the walls. They give the day's race card, form and tips. Television screens display lots of information, including the latest prices and the previous day's results. Pens are provided for the filling in of betting slips. The betting shop staff stand behind a counter and process bets and pay out winnings.

## Disadvantages of using a betting shop

### Late transmission of prices

A major problem with using betting shops is the lateness of the transmission of the prices from the racecourse. At the racecourse betting on the next race starts as soon as the previous race has finished. However, prices are not transmitted to the betting shops until around 15 minutes before the race, sometimes later. This delay can mean that you have missed out on more favourable prices. Big changes could have taken place in the prices, none of which you can see. The betting shops argue that they are waiting for a market to be formed and that they are not conning you out of money. However, if you were at the racecourse you would have had the opportunity to bet sooner.

As the off time of the race nears, betting on the lower-priced runners becomes more frantic. As more money pours on to them, their odds get shorter. The prices of the outsiders should become correspondingly bigger; however, in practice, they often do not. There simply is not time. On the course you can negotiate a price with the bookmaker, as he or she is independent. With the off-course bookmakers it is not possible to negotiate. The result is that the off-course bookmaker's profit increases.

## Writing a bet

Some betting shops have introduced machines for placing bets, however, in the vast majority of shops you need to write your bet on a betting slip.

Most bets are written on plain two-piece betting slips. You write on the top sheet and the bottom sheet is carbonized so it automatically makes a copy.

Some bets are written on special slips. These are common bets, such as lucky 15s, alphabets, union jack and tricast. Some bookmakers insist that a bet must be written on a certain type of slip to qualify for bonuses or consolations. It is therefore worth checking if the bet that you are making comes into this category.

Print everything in capital letters as the settler will need to be able to read what you have written, so the clearer the better. If the bookmaker cannot read it, he or she cannot settle it.

If you are making several bets, do not cram them all on to one slip. Use a separate slip for each. This not only makes settling your bet easier, it also makes it simpler for you to check that your bets are correctly staked.

The details you need to give on the bet are:

- the meeting and the time
- the name or race card number of your selection
- the instructions for the bet
- the stake
- the total stake

**Example bet**

| | |
|---|---|
| Ascot 2.30 | the meeting and the time |
| Dobbin | the name of the selection |
| £1 win | the instructions for the bet |
| Stake £1.00 | the stake |
| Total stake = £1.00 | the total stake |

## Time and meeting

It is important to include the time and meeting if you want your bet settled quickly. This applies even if you are betting on the next race. In busy betting shops where the settler has lots of bets to settle, untimed bets will usually be put to the bottom of the pile and dealt with after all the timed bets have been settled.

Forgetting to put the time of the race on your bet can cause problems if, instead of naming the horse, you just identify it by its race card number. You may intend betting on, for example, number 6 in the next horse race. However, if you do not time the bet and a greyhound race is run immediately after you place the bet, it will be settled on the result of the greyhound race.

Although it is more time-consuming, it is better to always write the horse's name to avoid this problem. Extra care should also be taken if there are two horses running with similar names.

## Mistakes on betting slips

It cannot be stressed enough that you should carefully check everything that you have written on your betting slip. Mistakes are all too common. The settler can only act upon what you have written on the slip and not on what you meant to write. The person who takes your bet is not responsible for checking it. He or she simply does not have the time to read every single bet that is placed. If you have any problems with a bet, the person to speak to is the shop manager. Any errors will be settled in accordance with the shop's rules.

## Placing a bet

Your completed slip should be handed to the cashier with the necessary money. The bet will not be processed until the money has been handed to the cashier.

You can pay with either cash or a cheque. Credit cards are not accepted. If you want to pay by cheque, you should inform the cashier at least 15 minutes before the start of the race, so that the cheque can be processed. If left any later the bet may be refused.

You have the option of either taking the price on offer at the time the bet is placed or having the bet settled at the starting price or tote odds. If you wish to take the current price on offer you should tell the cashier when you place your bet. The cashier will then mark the bet with the price and initial it. It is not acceptable to simply write the price on yourself and say nothing.

When a race is declared off, the cashier will process a slip through the till. Any bets taken after this 'off slip' will be void, win or lose. Try to get your bets on early because there is always a last-minute rush particularly on busy race days, such as Grand National day.

You can avoid the queues by betting early in the morning or even placing your bets the day before. Due to the huge number of bets placed on busy race days it can take some time before winnings can be collected. Unless you are desperate for your money, or enjoy queuing, it is better to collect your winnings during the following week.

## What happens if you lose your betting slip?

Unlike betting on the racecourse, there is no problem if you lose your betting slip. Because the bets are handwritten and everyone's handwriting is unique, your bet can soon be identified if you write out a copy of it. You will usually be required to fill in a form to claim the winnings. Small amounts will be paid out directly. For larger amounts you may have to produce some form of identification, such as a driver's licence.

## Bookmakers' rules

All bookmakers have a set of rules displayed in their shop. These cover such things as maximum payouts, what happens if an error is made on a bet and conditions that may apply to certain bets. The rules vary in different chains of shops, so if you are betting in a different shop then it is worth checking if the same conditions apply. Unfortunately, the rules tend to be full of jargon and not written in plain English. If you have any trouble interpreting them, the shop manager is the best person to ask.

## The weigh-in

After a race, the winning and placed jockeys have to weigh in to make sure that any weight they were carrying is correct. Most betting shops pay out winning bets, up to a certain amount, before the weigh-in. If a stewards' enquiry is announced, the result of the race may be amended. If you have collected your winnings and your horse is subsequently disqualified, you are not obliged to return the money to the bookmaker. If your horse was placed and is made the winner, the difference between what you have so far collected and what you are entitled to will be paid.

For betting purposes, once the weigh-in has been announced the result will stand regardless of subsequent events. Only very rarely will a result be amended after the weigh-in. This is usually if a horse has been positively tested for drugs. So if you are unfortunate enough to be on the horse that came second, you will not be paid out as a winner.

## Objections and stewards' enquiries

If an objection or a stewards' enquiry is called, the bookmaker will stop paying out on that race. The stewards will then look at the race and decide whether or not any rules have been broken. If the rules have been breached then the stewards may amend the result by disqualifying runners, altering the order of the placed horses, or voiding the race. It is therefore important not to throw away your betting slip until the runners have officially weighed in.

## Deposit/credit accounts

Most betting shops offer this service. It allows you to place bets over the telephone. Calls are recorded to minimize disputes. Deposit accounts allow you to deposit a certain amount of money with the betting shop and to place bets over the telephone up to the balance of your account. With credit accounts you are granted a certain amount of credit, which will depend on your financial circumstances. The main disadvantage with this method of betting is that the minimum stakes are higher than those in betting shops.

## Types of bets

Betting shops offer a wide variety of bets. Some of the most common are described below.

### Win single

One bet on the winner of a race.

### Each-way single

Two bets, one bet is for the selection to win and the other is for it to be placed. The place bet is settled as a fraction of the win odds. The number of places and the fraction of odds vary depending on how many runners there are and the type of race (see table).

**Number of places and fraction of odds paid for the place bet, determined by number of runners and type of race**

| Number of runners | Type of race | Number of places | Fraction of win odds |
|---|---|---|---|
| 16 or more | handicap | 4 | 1/4 |
| 12 to 15 | handicap | 3 | 1/4 |
| 8 to 15 | not applicable | 3 | 1/5 |
| 5 to 7 | not applicable | 2 | 1/4 |
| 4 or less | not applicable | 1 (win only) | both bets win |

### Double

A win double is one bet on two runners to win two different races. If the first selection wins, the returns are put on to the second selection.

An each-way double is two separate bets of a win double and a place double on two runners in two different races. The win bet is the same as a win double. For the place part of the bet, if the first selection is placed the returns become the stake for the second selection to be placed.

### Treble

One bet on three selections in three different races. If the first selection wins, the returns are put on to the second selection and if the second selection wins the returns are put on to the third selection.

### Accumulator

A bet on any number of selections, in different races, where the winnings on the first horse go on to the second and then on to the third and then on to the fourth and so on. It is one bet win, and two bets each-way. Obviously the returns can be quite large, depending on the prices of the winning selections. It is therefore worth checking that your winnings would not exceed the bookmaker's maximum payout.

### Straight forecast

Nominating which selections will finish first and second in the correct order.

### Reversed forecast

Nominating two selections to finish first and second in either order. It is two bets.

### Combination/full cover forecast

Selecting any number of runners in one race to finish first and second in either order. To calculate how may bets there are, simply multiply the number of selections by one number less.

- Three selections is 3 × 2 = 6 bets
- Four selections is 4 × 3 = 12 bets
- Five selections is 5 × 4 = 20 bets

### With the field forecast/against the field forecast

A forecast where the winner is nominated and any of the other runners in the race can be second. For example if you select Dobbin to win. You would write on the betting slip 'Dobbin to win against the field' or 'Dobbin to win with the field'.

Alternatively a selection can be nominated to finish second and for any of the other runners to win. This bet would be written as 'Dobbin to finish second against the field' or 'Dobbin to finish second with the field'.

To calculate the number of bets in both cases deduct one from the number of runners in the race. For a race with eight runners it is seven bets. For a race with ten runners it is nine bets.

### Tricast

Selecting three runners in the same race to finish first, second and third in the correct order.

### Trixie

Three selections in three different races, comprising three doubles and one treble. It is four bets win and eight bets each-way.

### Yankee

Four selections in four different races, comprising six doubles, four trebles and one fourfold. It is 11 bets win and 22 bets each-way.

### Mix

Similar to a yankee, except there are double the stakes on the fourfold. Four selections in four different races, comprising six doubles, four trebles and a double-staked fourfold. It is 11 bets but, as the fourfold is double staked the unit stake should be multiplied by 12 for win bets and 24 for each-way bets.

### Super yankee/canadian

Five selections in five different races, comprising ten doubles, ten trebles, five fourfolds and one fivefold. It is 26 bets win and 52 bets each-way.

### Heinz

Six selections in six different races, comprising 15 doubles, 20 trebles, 15 fourfolds, six fivefolds and one sixfold. It is 57 bets win and 114 bets each-way.

### Super heinz

Seven selections in seven different races, comprising 21 doubles, 35 trebles, 35 fourfolds, 21 fivefolds, seven sixfolds and one sevenfold. It is 120 bets win and 240 bets each-way.

### Goliath

Eight selections in eight different races, comprising 28 doubles, 56 trebles, 70 fourfolds, 56 fivefolds, 28 sixfolds, eight sevenfolds and one eightfold. It is 247 bets win and 494 bets each-way.

### Patent/twist

Three selections in three different races, comprising three singles, three doubles and one treble. There are seven bets win and 14 bets each-way.

### Perm patent 4

Four selections in four different races, comprising an individual patent on each group of three selections. It is 28 bets win and 56 bets each-way.

### Lucky 15

Four selections in four different races, comprising four singles, six doubles, four trebles and one fourfold. It is 15 bets win and 30 bets each-way. If there are four winners a 10 per cent bonus is paid, usually at the starting price. If there is only one winner, double the starting price odds are paid. These bonuses and consolations apply only to the win part of the bet. So, if an each-way lucky 15 has just one placed horse, double the odds is not paid on the placed selection. Similarly if one selection wins and one is a non-runner, the consolation is not paid.

### Lucky 31

Five selections in five different races, comprising five singles, ten doubles, ten trebles, five fourfolds and one fivefold. It is 31 bets win and 62 bets each-way.

The bonuses paid vary with different bookmakers. Some pay a bonus on four winners and five winners, others pay a bonus on only five winners. It is certainly worth shopping around to find the best offers. A consolation of double the starting price odds is paid for one winner.

### Lucky 63

Six selections in six different races, comprising six singles, 15 doubles, 20 trebles, 15 fourfolds, six fivefolds and one sixfold. It is 63 bets win and 126 bets each-way.

Bonuses vary with different bookmakers. A 10 per cent bonus is usually paid for five winners. For six winners the bonus is likely to be between 15 per cent and 25 per cent. A consolation of double starting price odds is paid for one winner.

### Any to come

Two selections in two different races (although more can be played). If the first selection wins, a stake equal to the original stake is placed on the second selection. It is also possible to specify an amount of stake for the second bet.

### Single stakes about/up and down bet

Two selections in two different races. If the first selection wins, an amount equal to the original stake is put on the second selection and vice versa. It is two bets.

### Double stakes about/double stakes up and down

As with the single stakes bet, except double the original stake is placed on the second selection and vice versa.

### Rounder

Three selections in three different races, in three bets win and six bets each-way. For selections A, B, C in a £1 rounder, the bets are as follows:

- £1 win A any to come £1 win double on the other two selections
- £1 win B any to come £1 win double on the other two selections
- £1 win C any to come £1 win double on the other two selections

### Roundabout

Three selections in three different races, in three bets. It is similar to a rounder, except double the original stakes are placed on the double.

For selections A, B, C in a £1 roundabout, the bets are as follows:

- £1 win A any to come £2 win double BC
- £1 win B any to come £2 win double AC
- £1 win C any to come £2 win double AB

### Round the clock

Any number of selections over three, in different races. It is one stake on the first selection any to come, one stake on the next selection any to come, one stake on the next selection. This continues on each selection. For three selections it is three bets, for four selections it is four bets and so on.

For selections A, B, C in a 10p win round the clock, the stake is 30p. The bets are as follows:

- 10p win A any to come 10p win B any to come 10p win C
- 10p win B any to come 10p win C any to come 10p win A
- 10p win C any to come 10p win A any to come 10p win B

### Round robin

Three selections in three different races, in three doubles, one treble and six single stakes about bets. It is ten bets win and 20 bets each-way.

For selections A, B, C the bets are as follows:

- doubles AB, AC, BC
- treble ABC
- single stakes about AB, AC, BC

### Flag

A bet on four selections in four different races, in a yankee, and 12 single stakes about bets. It is 28 bets win and 56 bets each-way.

### Super flag

A bet which consists of a super yankee and ten single stakes about bets. It is 46 bets win and 92 bets each-way.

## Internet betting

The innovation of the Internet has seen an explosion in the number of sites offering online betting. Some allow betting directly with credit cards, others require funds to be deposited by bank transfer.

The advantage to bettors is the convenience of being able to bet without leaving your home. There are, however, a number of disadvantages. The main problem with betting online is that it is unregulated and open to fraud. Many companies operate offshore to avoid taxation. This means that disputes are not easily solved.

If you want to bet online, it is best only to bet with a well-known company. If you want to bet in this manner, find the web site's address from an offline source, as it is easy for unscrupulous operators to fake web sites so that they appear to be run by a well-known company.

In the USA, gambling over the Internet is illegal under the federal Wire Communications Act, which prohibits the use of interstate telephone lines for transmitting bets or betting information. Prosecutions have already been initiated against operators of Internet betting services.

## Betting over the telephone

In many countries it is possible to bet over the telephone. The types of account vary. Some bookmakers offer credit. Others insist on a sum of money being deposited with them before you can bet. The minimum bets with these accounts tend to be for relatively higher stakes. When you phone the company your call will be recorded to avoid disputes.

# 03 understanding the odds

**In this chapter you will learn:**

- how bookmaking works
- how to get a good price
- about factors that affect prices.

Crucial to betting on horse racing is an understanding of the odds or prices. The odds or prices give an indication of your potential winnings and whether or not a bet is worthwhile making. There are a huge variety of different types of odds and prices, and a lot of slang expressions are used to describe the odds. Sometimes you may take a price but certain conditions may mean that this price is altered. The occurrence of dead heats, withdrawn horses and joint favourites may mean you are paid out less than you expected. The following should give you a better understanding of what kind of bet to make and what you can hope to win from it.

## Bookmaking

### How the prices are determined

A bookmaker uses an expert called a handicapper to assess the chances of each runner in the race. The handicapper will consider a number of factors to determine the chances of each horse, such as pedigree, recent performance, the jockey, weight carried and the condition of the ground. A book of prices is then made depending on the assessment. The runner that the handicapper thinks is most likely to win will have the lowest price and is called the favourite. Occasionally two runners are deemed to have an equal chance of winning. They will have the same price and be called joint favourites. If several runners have the same lowest price they are called co-favourites.

The prices of the horses in a race can vary enormously. Just because a horse has a large price it does not necessarily mean that it will not win. For example, in 1990 Equinoctial won at Kelso at a staggering price of 250/1 – the longest odds ever recorded in British horse racing.

The initial prices offered are called tissue prices. This is just a preliminary indication of the prices and they tend to be a conservative estimate of a horse's chance of winning. Once bets have been made the prices are said to have been laid. This means a betting market has been made. The prices then change depending on how much money is bet.

The prices do not show the chances that a horse has of winning. Instead they reflect how much money has been bet on them. The horse attracting the greatest amount of money in bets will have the lowest price. The horse attracting the least amount of money will have the highest price. Horses with high prices are called outsiders or rags.

### Bar

When prices are quoted for a race, the odds for some outsiders may not be given. Instead a bar price is shown. This means that all the horses not quoted in the betting are at a higher price than that given in the bar. For example in a ten-runner race, prices may be given for seven of the runners and a bar price of 25/1. This means that the other three horses all have a price of greater than 25/1. If you want to place a bet on one of the unquoted horses, you will need to agree a price with the bookmaker.

## Understanding the odds

When you go to place a bet, you will see that there are prices (odds) quoted for the runners. These prices are usually made up of two numbers with a slash between, for example 5/4, 11/8, 5/1, 7/2, 15/2, 25/1. These prices are a ratio telling you what you will win for a particular stake. The amount on the left of the price is what you will win if you bet the amount on the right. The money bet is called the stake. If you win, your stake is refunded. The total amount won is called the returns or payout.

**Examples**

If the price quoted is 6/1, you will win £6 for every £1 staked. Your stake is also refunded. If you bet £5 on a horse at 6/1, your returns will be $(6 \times 5) + 5 = £35$.

If you bet £4 on a horse at odds of 6/4, your returns will be $6 + 4 = £10$.

If you bet £1 on a horse at odds of 11/2 your returns will be $5.5 + 1 = £6.50$.

### Odds against and odds on

Where the number on the left of the price is bigger than the number on the right the term 'odds against' is used; where it is less it is called 'odds on'. Where both numbers are the same, that is, 1/1, the term 'even money' or 'evens' is used.

**Examples**

1/1 is even money (always written as 'evens').

13/8 is odds against, 8/13 is odds on.

5/2 is odds against, 2/5 is odds on.

You will often hear prices quoted with the word 'on', for example, '2/1 on'. This actually means that the price is 1/2. Therefore when the word 'on' is quoted, to find the correct price the order of the price needs to be reversed. '11/8 on' is 8/11, '7/4 on' is 4/7, and '6/5 on' is 5/6. This can lead to confusion, particularly if you mishear. When prices are announced in betting shops they are given in the correct order.

## Each-way

Bookmakers also accept each-way bets. This is two bets. One bet is for the horse to win the race and the other is for it to be placed second, third or fourth. The number of places paid depends on the number of runners in the race (see the table on page 33). It is important to pay particular attention to the number of places paid as some bookmakers offer lower odds than others.

**Example**

Suppose you bet £10 each-way on a horse. Your stake will be £20 because an each-way bet is two bets. If the horse wins at 4/1 and ¼ of the odds are paid for the place:

The win part of the bet pays $(4 \times 10) + 10 = £50$.

The place part of the bet pays only ¼ the odds of the win. To find the correct odds to calculate the returns you need to multiply the number on the right of the price by 4. (If the bet was at 1/5 odds you would need to multiply by 5.)

So the win odds of 4/1 become place odds of 4/4 (which is evens – 1/1). So the place part pays $(1 \times 10) + 10 = £20$.

The total returns are £50 + £20 = £70.

If your horse wins the race, one bet will be settled at the full odds but the other bet will be settled at a fraction of the odds.

If the horse were to come second, the win bet would be lost but the place bet would be won. The returns would be £20.

In races where there are four runners or less, it is not possible to bet each-way. It is only possible to bet on the winner. If an each-way bet is placed, all the stakes go on the horse to win. This is called 'all up' and is often abbreviated to 'Au'.

## Tic-tac

The bookmakers at the racecourse use a system of hand signals called tic-tac to communicate prices and bets made to one another. At the racecourse you will often hear slang used for the prices:

- jolly – favourite
- evens – levels
- 11/10 tips
- 5/4 wrist
- 11/8 up the arm
- 6/4 ear 'ole
- 7/4 shoulder
- 15/8 double tops
- 2/1 bottle
- 5/2 face
- 11/4 elef a vier
- 3/1 carpet
- 100/30 burlington bertie
- 4/1 rouf
- 5/1 hand
- 9/2 on the shoulders
- 6/1 exes
- 7/1 neves
- 9/1 enin
- 10/1 cockle
- 11/1 elef
- 12/1 net and bice
- 14/1 net and rouf
- 16/1 net and ex
- 20/1 double net
- 25/1 macaroni
- 25/1 pony
- 33/1 double carpet
- 100/1 century

Once a bookmaker has decided what his initial prices are, he will offer them to the punters. As money is bet, the bookmaker calculates his or her liability should that selection win. If the book does not balance with the prices currently on offer, the bookmaker will adjust the prices accordingly.

When a bet is placed the bookmaker will call out the winnings to the stake that has been bet and give a ticker to the punter. There are no details of the bet marked on the ticket. Instead it is just marked with a number that corresponds to an entry in the bookmaker's ledger. The bookmaker's clerk will enter the bet into the ledger. The ledger will have a section for each runner. The details that are kept are the stakes and winnings on each bet, the cumulative stakes and winnings, and the punter's ticket number. A running total of the stakes is also kept.

By comparing the cumulative stake with the total stakes, the bookmaker can easily see what his or her liabilities are. If any of the cumulative stake figures exceed the total stakes, then the prices on those runners need to be reduced. The runners where the liabilities are less than the total stakes can have their prices lengthened.

**Example**

If we look at two of the runners in a race, the prices on offer may be as follows: runner A 1/4; runner B 2/1.

Suppose the following bets were made:

**1** £40 win A.
**2** £20 win B.
**3** £20 win A.
**4** £5 win B.

By comparing the total stake to the cumulative winnings on each runner, the liability can be calculated (see table below).

**Bookmaker's ledger for recording bets**

**Selection A**

| a | b | c | d | e |
|---|---|---|---|---|
| 50 | 10 | 40 | 40 | 1 |
| 75 | 5 | 20 | 60 | 3 |

**Selection B**

| a | b | c | d | e |
|---|---|---|---|---|
| 60 | 40 | 20 | 20 | 2 |
| 75 | 10 | 5 | 25 | 4 |

a = cumulative returns
b = returns
c = stake
d = cumulative stake
e = ticket number

| Total stake | If A wins | If B wins |
|---|---|---|
| 1 40 | lose £10 | win £40 |
| 2 60 | win £10 | break even |
| 3 80 | win £5 | break even |
| 4 85 | win £10 | break even |

At this stage, the bookmaker may decide to shorten the price on B in order to increase his profit.

# Are you being offered a good price?

When you assess your horse, make an estimate about what price it should be in the betting. How does your estimate compare to its actual price? Are you getting value for money?

## Fixed odds in betting shops

Fixed odds betting shops, often called bookies, operate in countries including Great Britain and Ireland. There are major chains of betting shops run by large companies, and many independent operators. Betting shops offer a wide variety of different types of prices and bets. They operate in a similar way to bookmakers by offering prices at fixed odds. Some of their prices are determined by what the on-course bookmakers are offering. Other prices are decided by the betting shops themselves. Some are only available at certain times.

## Ante-post prices

When a bet is placed before the day of the event it is called an ante-post bet. For major races, such as the Grand National and the Derby, prices are available many months before they are run.

The prices are normally more favourable than those offered on the day of the event. However, if your runner is withdrawn from the race, your stake is automatically lost.

Sometimes there are too many horses entered for a race. For safety reasons only a certain number may run. In this situation a procedure called balloting out will determine which horses run. If your runner is balloted out, your stakes will be refunded. The prices of the remaining horses will be adjusted according to rule 4 (see page 50).

Although ante-post betting has its risks, such as horses being withdrawn, the benefit of the higher prices is usually advantageous to the punter.

## Early morning prices

Most betting shops offer prices on several races as soon as they open for business. These are usually on the handicap races but some may give prices on all the races. These prices are quite often advertised in the sporting press. It is worthwhile comparing the prices offered by different operators, as they will vary.

As soon as betting starts on the race the prices will change. Some betting shops will not change the early prices for a certain amount of time after they open for business. This allows customers to take the prices as advertised in the press. Some also guarantee that if their early morning prices are worse than the starting prices, the bet will be settled at the starting price. If you want to take the early morning prices you should place your bet as early as possible. The prices will only be available up to the first show.

The races will be running the same day, so if your selection does not run, your stake will be refunded.

## Board prices/shows

Around ten minutes before the race starts prices will be passed from the racecourse. The prices represent an average of what the bookmakers on the course are offering. Once the betting shop has received these prices, the early morning prices can no longer be taken. The board prices will change continually as money is bet on the runners up to the start of the race. Each new set of prices that is transmitted is called a show. The first set of prices transmitted is called the first show. The name 'board prices' comes from the old custom of writing the prices on a board in the betting shop. Nowadays the prices appear on television screens. As well as the current price on offer, the previous shows are also given. The current price is the one that is furthest to the right. As the start of the race approaches, the prices change with greater frequency.

## Starting prices

Usually abbreviated to SP, the starting prices are an average of the prices that a sample of on-course bookmakers are offering at the start of the race, as agreed by the starting price executive. The starting price executive is made up of three major media companies, the Press Association, Trinity Mirror and Satellite Information Services. They employ starting price returners who make a note of prices offered in the betting ring for all the horses in each race, just before the off. An average of these prices is used to calculate the starting price.

When the results of the races are published in the press, the starting prices will be quoted. If you have taken a price like an early price or ante-post price, then your bet will be settled as the odds taken, regardless of the starting price. If you do not take a price then your bet will be settled at the starting price. In the event that no prices are quoted, the bets will be settled using the tote dividends.

## Tote dividends

Tote dividends are quoted by the official tote on the racecourse. Most bookmakers take bets on the tote and will have a sign stating that they are authorized to take them. For bets at tote odds there are dividends quoted to a £1 stake for win, place, forecast, tricast, placepots and jackpots.

When placing a tote bet with a betting shop it is important to clearly mark 'TOTE' on the betting slip. Failure to do so will result in the bet being settled at the starting price.

When you place a tote bet in a betting shop your money does not go into the pool. The betting shop simply allows you the convenience of betting on the prices that will be attained by these markets. If you place a tote bet, you have no idea what is currently in the pools at the racecourse.

The dividends returned can vary quite considerably from the starting prices. This tends to happen more frequently at minor race meetings where the betting market is not strong. The problem with placing a tote bet in a betting shop is that you do not get the full benefit if the tote returns are much better than the starting prices. Most betting shops place a limit on how much they will pay on the tote, relative to the starting price. The maximum can be as much as four times the starting price equivalent, but may be much lower. However, you will often be guaranteed a minimum payout; a minimum of half the starting price equivalent is common.

Large tote bets placed in betting shops are subject to scrutiny as they are often used in betting coups. At a race meeting with a poor attendance, the betting market can be weak. This makes it easier to manipulate. If you bet at the track, your bet goes into the tote and reduces the dividend for that horse. Relatively small bets can completely alter the dividends and return an artificially high dividend on one horse. If this horse is backed with tote bets in a betting shop, these bets do not affect the eventual tote dividend. If the horse wins, the dividend is artificially high.

## Forecast and tricast

These are quoted to a £1 stake from the racecourse. Sometimes bookmakers may offer their own forecast prices, most commonly for foreign racing, where a dividend may not be given from the racecourse.

## Betting on foreign racing

With the innovation of satellite transmission of racing, it is becoming more common for coverage to be given for major foreign racing. Simulcasting allows bettors in another country to bet directly into the pools at a foreign racecourse. An example of this is betting on the Breeders' Cup and the Prix de l'Arc de Triomphe which allowed British bettors to bet on the tote at the racecourse

If you bet in British betting shops on French racing you have the choice of betting on the pari-mutuel (French tote) or with the betting shop's prices. It is not possible to predict what is better, but at least if you take a price you know in advance what your winnings will be. If you take the betting shop's prices you have to pay tax at 9 per cent. Also, if you combine pari-mutuel bets with SP (starting price) bets in a multiple bet, you will pay tax.

### Pari-mutuel dividends

Pari-mutuel is the name of the French horse racing tote. The dividends are quoted to a FF1 stake and there is no need to pay tax on the stake as it is deducted at the racecourse before the dividend is announced.

One major difference with the French system of betting is the coupling of horses. If horses from the same stable are running in the same race, then the same price for those horses will be given in the betting. The horses are said to be coupled. A bet on one horse from that stable is also a bet on any one of the other horses from the same stable. Therefore, if horses A and B are coupled, and a £1 win is placed on horse A, the bet will also win if horse B wins.

If, however, you take the betting shop's price on a horse, your horses will not be coupled.

### Prices given in newspapers

When a newspaper prints the racecards, they will usually quote prices for the runners. These are a guide only as to what the particular newspaper expects the starting prices to be. They will vary from paper to paper. It is not possible to take these prices.

## Factors affecting prices

Even though you may have taken a price, the odds at which your bet is settled may be adjusted if certain conditions apply.

### Non-runners

A non-runner is a horse that does not take part in the race. A horse may be withdrawn any time up to the off of a race. If you bet on a non-runner on the day of the race, your stake will be refunded. If you bet ante-post, you will lose your stake.

If a horse comes under starters orders in a race but refuses to run, it is not considered a non-runner. It is important to check the results because a horse can be withdrawn right up to the last minute. You may see it set off for the start, but it may, for example, be withdrawn because it refuses to go into the starting stalls.

# Withdrawn horses

## Rule 4 deductions

After a book has been made on a race, a horse may be withdrawn. This will mean that the prices offered on the race will be incorrect, as they would have been worked out including the withdrawn horse. The bookmakers are therefore allowed to make an adjustment to the prices, called a rule 4 deduction (usually abbreviated to R4). The deduction is quoted as an amount in the pound, for example 10 pence in the pound. The amount of the deduction is determined by the price of the withdrawn horse (see table below). The deduction applies to both winning and placed horses. Only the winnings are affected and not your stake.

**Rule 4 deductions**

| Odds of horse withdrawn | | Deduction | % of winnings |
|---|---|---|---|
| 3/10 or shorter | | 75p in £ | 75 |
| Over 3/10 | up to and including 2/5 | 70p in £ | 70 |
| Over 2/5 | up to and including 8/15 | 65p in £ | 65 |
| Over 8/15 | up to and including 8/13 | 60p in £ | 60 |
| Over 8/13 | up to and including 4/5 | 55p in £ | 55 |
| Over 4/5 | up to and including 20/21 | 50p in £ | 50 |
| Over 20/21 | up to and including 6/5 | 45p in £ | 45 |
| Over 6/5 | up to and including 6/4 | 40p in £ | 40 |
| Over 6/4 | up to and including 7/4 | 35p in £ | 35 |
| Over 7/4 | up to and including 9/4 | 30p in £ | 30 |
| Over 9/4 | up to and including 3/1 | 25p in £ | 25 |
| Over 3/1 | up to and including 4/1 | 20p in £ | 20 |
| Over 4/1 | up to and including 11/2 | 15p in £ | 15 |
| Over 11/2 | up to and including 9/1 | 10p in £ | 10 |
| Over 9/1 | up to and including 14/1 | 5p in £ | 5 |
| Over 14/1 | | no deduction | |

**Example**

A horse that was 4/1 in the betting is withdrawn. The SP of the winning horse is 2/1. The price will be subject to a rule 4 deduction of 20p in the £.

A £10 bet tax paid on a winning horse at 2/1 would normally return £30. With a rule 4 deduction of 20p in the £, the bet would return £26.

Calculation: (20 – 20%) + 10 = 26

If there is sufficient time before the race is off, a new book will be made. In this case, the rule 4 deduction will apply to prices taken before the time that the new book was made. Prices taken on the new book and SP prices will not be subject to a rule 4 deduction.

### Each-way bets

Horses being withdrawn can also affect the odds paid and the number of places paid for each-way bets. When you placed your bet there may have been eight runners, meaning you would expect to be paid if your horse came third. However, if a horse is withdrawn the third placed horse no longer counts, as there will only be seven runners. You will only get paid if your horse is first or second.

## Dead heats

Occasionally two horses or more are declared the winner. This is a dead heat. When a horse dead-heats for first place, the returns are halved. If there are three horses in the dead heat, then the returns are divided by three. If placed horses dead-heat, the returns are only reduced if there are more places that usual being paid. For example, if two horses dead-heat for second place and three places would normally be paid, the returns will not be affected. If, however, only two places would normally be paid and two horses dead-heat for second place, the returns of the placed horses will be affected. So, too, will the returns of any each-way bets on the winner.

## Unnamed favourites

The favourite is the runner with the lowest price. It is possible to bet on the favourite without actually naming it. However, it is possible for more than one runner to be the favourite. If two runners have the same lowest price they are called joint favourites. Should there be several runners with the lowest prices, they are called co-favourites. Should an unnamed favourite win (that is, you have just written the favourite to win on your betting slip), the returns will be divided by however many favourites there are. Since prices can change very quickly, the starting prices can differ hugely between when you first place your bet and when the starting prices are returned. If you intend to bet on a particular horse, it is much better to name it on your slip.

## Tax

There is no tax deducted from bets at British and Irish racecourses. However, if you place a bet in an Irish betting shop, your bets will be subject to tax (see page 75). Betting tax was abolished in Britain in 2001.

## Payout exceeds the bookmaker's limit

Bookmakers place limits on how much they will pay out. For the larger chains of bookmakers the limits are high. Small bookmakers have much lower limits. Before you place a large bet, you should check that your potential payout does not exceed this limit. It is worthless placing, for example, a £100 bet if a £50 bet is sufficient to reach the payout limit.

# 04 making your selection

**In this chapter you will learn:**

- **how to assess the runners**
- **where to find information about the runners**
- **about betting systems.**

Deciding which horse to bet on in a race is not easy. Many factors influence the outcome of horse races, including the jockey, the weight carried, the condition of the ground and the distance of the race. This makes betting on horse racing both interesting and challenging. A gambler needs to use his or her skill to assess the likely winner and/or placed horses from a field of up to 40 runners.

Even after taking into account all the different factors, some aspects of horse racing are unpredictable. No matter how carefully you have assessed a horse's chances of winning, something can go wrong which can affect the outcome of a race. In national hunt races, horses can be brought down by others, they may slip on wet ground, or the weights carried by the horse may be lost in the course of the race, causing the horse to be disqualified. Even the jockey's actions may result in a horse being disqualified. Races are run at a fast pace with the jockey making split-second decisions. His or her actions can result in other horses being impeded, which may lead to disqualification. In his or her eagerness to make a horse win, the jockey may use the whip more frequently than is allowed under the rules.

A great deal of the information that you need to consider when assessing a horse's chance of winning is given by the race cards printed in newspapers and programmes. The format varies depending on the publication. To save space abbreviations are used.

The analysis of all of this information is very time-consuming. In recent years a number of computer programs have been developed to process this information, and help cut down on the work. There are many different programs on the market, all offering different features, so it is worth shopping around for the best deal.

A wealth of information is now available on the Internet. The amount of information is almost overwhelming. Lots of online racing magazines, horse racing web sites and tipsters services now exist. Many provide up-to-date analysis of all the statistics, such as the performance of favourites, the influence of the draw, the top trainers, the top jockeys and pedigree information.

# Factors you can assess

## Pedigree

For all racehorses it is possible to trace back their pedigrees for hundreds of years. A good pedigree is an indication of a potentially good horse, but not always. Horses are carefully bred to bring out characteristics that make good runners. Horses with good racing records are sent to stud in order to try to bring out those characteristics in future generations. However, due to the nature of genetics, the breeding of these characteristics is not always an exact science. A dam and sire with good racing records do not always produce fast offspring. Often the characteristics that make a good runner can skip generations.

One characteristic that has been shown to have a positive affect on the performance of horses is a large heart. Although this characteristic may be present in the sire it may not show up in his immediate offspring, only to reappear in later generations.

This can mean that a horse that may have had a poor racing record can sire fast offspring. This makes the study of pedigree an inexact method of finding winners. It tends to be used as a tool for finding winners where the horses have not run before.

## Previous performance of the runners

Due to the unpredictability of breeding, a great deal of importance is placed on the previous performance of a horse. Once the horse has actually run, you have a clearer indication of its potential, and information is available on how the horses have performed in previous races. This is called 'form'. Different racing publications publish this information in different formats. To cut down on space, many abbreviations are used and each publication will give a key explaining them. As a general rule, the more detailed the information, the more you have to pay for it. You will therefore need to decide for yourself how important you feel the information is. The types of details that are given are the results of previous races, the jockey, trainer, weight carried and a guide to the betting. When the horse has not run in many races in the current season, its performance for the previous season will be given.

Try to watch as many races as possible. The written data does not always show why a horse performed poorly. The jockey may have been at fault. He or she may have waited too long before pushing a horse. A horse may sprint quickly at the end of the race but if the jockey left it too late to push or was boxed in by other horses, it may still lose. A better jockey next time out may compensate.

Some horses may have an easy win, with the jockeys not having to use the whip or, alternatively, easing down near the finish. Other horses may win but only under pressure from the jockey. A poorer jockey next time out may mean the horse loses. A horse could fall at a difficult fence. If the fences are easier in its next race, the horse may not be so unfortunate. In sprinting races a horse may get off to a bad start. The next race may be better.

## Speed of the horse

The speed that a horse can run at is by far the clearest indication of how likely a horse is to win. No matter how good the jockey, the trainer or the condition of the ground, if a horse is not fast it is unlikely to win. Assessing the speed is not a simple matter. Factors such as the amount of weight carried and the going all affect a horse's speed.

*Timeform* offer the most comprehensive records of the speed of horses. They produce a daily newspaper and separate books giving details of flat racing and national hunt statistics. For anyone seriously assessing a horse's chances of winning, this information is invaluable. You can, of course, accumulate the information yourself if you are prepared to commit the time it takes to gather the data.

## Harness racing

The United States Trotting Association keeps records of the fastest race a horse wins each year. Abbreviations are used to cut down on space. With harness racing the comparison of the runners is made much easier as most races are run over a mile.

**Example: p,3,Q1:58.1($100,000)**

p – the horse gait p=pace, no letter = trot.

3 – age of the horse, here it was a 3-year-old.

Q – the type of race. Q = qualifying race, T = time trial, no letter = during a race.

1:58.1 – the time taken to run one mile, in this case one minute and fifty-eight and one-fifth seconds.

the length of the track. f = ⅝ mile, s = ⅞ mile, h = ½ mile, no letter = 1 mile

($100,000) – the amount of money won by the horse in its career.

## The distance of the race

Most horses have an optimum distance over which they perform well. Some are excellent sprinters while others have stamina to cope with longer distances. If a horse is entered for a distance that it has never run before, its previous performance can provide some indication as to how well it will fare. Has the horse run shorter distances and won easily? Or has it run longer distances but lacked stamina and faded at the end. If you watch lots of racing you will notice these factors.

## Change of class

The grade of race may have an effect on the outcome of a race. For example, if a horse performs particularly well in a group 2 race, it may be entered for a group 1 race. Since group 1 races attract the best horses, it will be up against much stronger opposition than in its previous race. It is also possible for horses to drop down a grade so a horse that has previously run in a group 1 race may compete in a group 2 race. The horse may have performed badly in the group 1 race but the change of class may lead to a huge improvement. The form guides in newspapers give details of which horses are running in different classes.

## Experience of the runners

It is notoriously difficult to pick winners in races where the horses have never run before. The problem with betting on them is that you have no previous form on which to base your assessment. This is where the pedigree of the horse needs to be studied. You can glean the horse's potential by studying the racing records of its parents, the dam and sire. They may also have produced other offspring that have already run which gives you more information on which to base your selection. The trainer, jockey and owner will also play a role in your selection.

A horse's experience can be particularly important over jumps. An inexperienced horse that has only recently been trained to jump is more likely to fall than one with more experience.

Flat races, where the horses must start in stalls, can cause problems. Experienced horses are more used to the stalls and less likely to be nervous. A nervous horse can easily injure itself and/or the jockey in the stalls, or simply refuse to race once it has been let out. You will also know of experienced horses that are nervous in the stalls.

Although an older horse has more experience, it may also be less fit than its rivals. You will need to decide at what stage the age of a horse becomes a negative factor. This is not always easy as some horses do have exceptional records even at an old age. Red Rum was 12 years old when he won his third Grand National. In 1980 Sonny Somers won two steeplechases at the age of 18. The record for the oldest horse ever to win a flat race is held by Marksman who won at Ashford in 1826 at the age of 18.

## The condition of the ground

The condition of the ground on the racecourse is called 'the going'. Before the start of racing, the clerk of the course will inspect the condition of the ground and declare the going. The going is classified from the fastest to the slowest conditions as follows:

- hard
- firm
- good to firm
- good
- good to soft
- soft/yielding
- heavy

Since the courses do not drain evenly there may be patches of ground where the going differs from the rest of the course. For example, you may see the going quoted as 'good (good to firm patches)'. In order to get more consistent ground, some tracks are watered. On all-weather tracks, where the racing surface is made of fibre-sand, the going is fairly consistent and is quoted as 'standard'.

The condition of the ground may affect how some horses run. For example, some run well on heavy ground, while others run poorly. If you attend a race meeting, you will able to inspect the ground yourself and draw your own conclusions about how it will affect the horses.

A good time for betting can be towards the end of the flat season when the ground has usually dried out. This removes one of the unknown factors. Also by this stage the performance of the horses is known. This is traditionally a time of year when the bookmakers start losing money.

## The jockey

The experience and recent performance of the jockey will have an impact on your selection. Watch out for changes to the jockey which may result if a jockey is injured.

## The course

In the USA the racetracks are of less importance, as they are mostly the same oval-shaped dirt tracks. In Great Britain, where the courses are all different, this can also have an effect on how well a horse runs. Some courses have left-hand bends and others right. Some are flat, while others have slight inclines and some steep hills.

You will need to consider how the racecourse is going to affect a horse. The horse you select may have a preference for right-hand turns; therefore, you will need to assess the impact of a course with left-hand turns. A horse may run well on a flat course, but how is a hill going to affect its performance?

Starting stalls are used in flat racing to ensure that each horse starts at precisely the same time. The draw is the position in which the horse starts in the stalls – not to be confused with its race card number. At a lot of racecourses there are advantages to starting in certain positions in the stalls. The list on pages 66–8 details the effect of the draw.

## Weather conditions

Always take note of the weather forecast. If it is expected to rain, bear in mind that the going may change. Some horses fare better than others depending on the weather conditions. Hot weather has a more adverse effect on big horses than on small ones.

## Blinkers

Some horses are distracted by other horses and do not run well. Blinkers are an aid that allow a horse only to see in front of it, so that the other runners are excluded from its vision. If a horse is wearing blinkers for the first time, there might be a marked improvement in its running.

## The condition of the horse

In the course of racing and training horses may get injured. Nowadays veterinary care is of the highest quality with excellent treatment available. The effect of an injury on a horse's future performance can be negligible. However, some horses may have recurrent injury problems that can make their performance unreliable. Keeping up-to-date with all the news will highlight any horses that are not entirely fit.

Pregnancy can be a big advantage to a horse. This is due to an increase in red blood cells which allows more oxygen to be carried to the muscles and so increases their efficiency, meaning a horse can run much faster.

## The owner

The owner of a horse can also be included in your assessment. Some owners have particularly good reputations for spotting and buying good-quality horses with the potential to win races. Your knowledge about owners can also help with the selection of horses on their first outings. If a particular owner has a good record of winners, a horse on its first outing entered in a race by that owner may have a better chance of winning than novices of other owners.

## The trainer

All trainers are different. They employ a variety of methods for training horses – some are better than others. Some trainers also have good reputations for bringing out the very best in a horse. You will need to keep up-to-date with the latest news to discover which trainers are producing winners. Another important factor is a change of trainer. A better trainer may improve the performance of a horse.

# Factors you cannot assess

Because horse racing is unpredictable, things can and do go wrong. All the studying in the world cannot guard against them.

## Horses can have off days too

Horses can be unpredictable. Even the most well-behaved horses can have off days. If they do not want to co-operate with a jockey they will:

- dig their heels in and refuse to run
- not go into the starting stall
- refuse to jump fences
- attempt to throw off a jockey

You may know in advance that a horse has a reputation for being difficult, so it is best to avoid betting on it. Save your money for the runners you are certain of.

## Other horses

It is common for horses to bring down others at jumps. A horse may be the best jumper in the world but, if another horse gets in its way, it can easily fall. Loose horses can cause all sorts of problems. They can box in your selection, bump into it or run across its path, all of which can cause a horse to lose a race.

## Weights

Weights can and do occasionally fall off during the course of a race. Jockeys also sometimes forget to weigh in after a race. Either of these situations results in disqualification.

## False starts

A false start can ruin a horse's chance of winning – it may have run half of the race before being recalled. However, safeguards have been put in place to prevent a repeat performance of the 1993 British Grand National fiasco when several horses completed the course after a false start.

## Other factors

Jockeys do occasionally take the wrong course. Horses can also escape from the jockey before the race. This can result in them being withdrawn from the race, particularly if they have used up a lot of energy running all over the course. Although you will have your stake refunded (unless, you have bet ante-post – see pages 45–6) if that horse is your selection, it can mean your hard work has been wasted. Alternatively, if your horse is still running, it can mean that adjustments to the betting make your bet unprofitable (if, for example, you have bet each-way).

Although these incidents do not happen frequently, you should bear them in mind as possibilities. It is tempting to stake a lot of money on a horse when you think it cannot fail to win. By keeping your stakes to a reasonable level on each race, you will minimize your losses when these events do occur.

## Gathering information

A great deal of information is given by the race cards printed in newspapers or programmes. The format varies depending on the publication. To save space many abbreviations are used.

**Example race card**

2.00 Winner's Stakes £3,752 (4 run)

| | | | | | |
|---|---|---|---|---|---|
| 1(2) | 2/1-132 | Liberty Dawn (14) (B, CD) | J Jones | 5 11 4 | J Smith |
| 2(3) | | Bronze Cannon | F Evans | 4 10 10 | D Bolton |
| 3(1) | 111 | Lucky Luc (28) | S Moon | 4 10 10 | S Heard |
| 4(4) | | Suzie's Boy | G Chip | 5 11 4 | K Bearman |

Betting: 2 Lucky Luc, 4 Liberty Dawn, 10 Bronze Cannon, Suzie's Boy.

2.00 – time of the race
Winner's Stakes – name of the race
£3,752 – prize money to the winning owner
(4 run) – number of runners
1 – race card number
(2) – draw – position in starting stalls
01-132 – the horse's form in its last six races
1 =1st, 2 = 2nd, 3 = 3rd, 0 = unplaced, d = disqualified
A dash (-) is a break of one season. An oblique (/) indicates two or more seasons' break. The figure on the right is the latest race. In national hunt racing the following abbreviations are also used: U = unseated rider; F = fell; B = brought down; P = pulled up; R = refused.
Liberty Dawn – the name of the horse
(14) – number of days since it last ran
(B, CD) – meanings of abbreviations follow:
B = horse was wearing blinkers, headgear that restricts lateral vision

V = visor, blinkers that minimize awareness of activity on either side
H = a hood
E = eyeshield
B* = blinkers worn for the first time
BF = beaten favourite last time out
C = winner over the course
D = winner over the distance

| | |
|---|---|
| CD | – course and distance winner |
| J Jones | – name of trainer |
| Betting | – rough guide to what the betting is likely to be |
| 5 11 4 | – a 5-year-old horse, carrying 11 stone 4 |
| J Smith | – name of the jockey |

## Learn about horse racing

Become knowledgeable about horse racing. Read as many publications as possible. Ensure that you have a thorough understanding of the subject. Keep up-to-date with the latest news by reading a good-quality racing newspaper. The more information you have, the better able you are to assess a horse's chance of winning.

## Tipsters

Studying all these factors takes an enormous amount of time. If you lack the time to do it yourself there are other people who have already done all of the hard work. They are the tipsters employed by the newspapers. They select the likely prospects that they think will win.

However, you do not know what system they are using to assess the horses and how good that system is. They may have missed an important factor that you may have noticed. The newspapers boast when their tipsters get it right but keep quiet when they do not – after all they are in the business of selling newspapers. Over the course of the year tipsters get it wrong too.

## Record predictors

The record for predicting the most winners in one day is held by Charles Lamb, racing correspondent for the *Baltimore News American*. In 1974, he picked out ten winners at a meeting held at Delaware Park, USA. In Great Britain, Bob Butcher of the

*Daily Mirror* correctly forecast seven winners for a meeting at Wolverhampton. So, too, did Fred Shawcross at a York meeting in 1988.

# Systems

Looking through the small ads of publications will often turn up a number of advertisements for betting systems. There are many different systems. They often guarantee excellent returns.

Do they work? The sellers of systems will tell you they do. Friends will boast that they have invented the ultimate system that never fails. Throughout the years many systems have been invented, some more successful than others.

Ignore all the claims that are made about a system. To test how effective it is, try it out yourself on a dummy run. Do not bet any money. Make a note of results over a period of time and apply the system to those results. If it gives good returns then try it with small stakes. Continue to monitor results. If it starts failing then give up on it and try something else.

## Developing your own systems for selecting horses

Try to develop your own systems for selecting horses to bet on. You will need to take account of all the influencing factors mentioned. Some are more important than others but all play a part. One method is to award points for each factor. Most importance should be placed on the speed of a horse, with points added for factors that have a positive influence and points deducted for those that have a negative influence.

## Doubling up on the favourite

Some systems involve no assessment of the runners. A popular system is doubling up on the favourite. Here, a bet is placed on the favourite in the first race. If that loses, the stake is doubled and placed on the favourite in the second race. This continues until there is a winner and the gambler stops betting.

This system falls down in several ways. The capital required to make it work can be huge. It may be some time before a favourite wins (they lose around 60 per cent of their races). You also need to make allowances for tax if you place your bets in a betting shop. If the favourite is a very low price (below 6/5) you will not recoup your outlay. There is always the danger that a horse could be withdrawn. This could bring the price of the favourite below the level that you need to break even. The potential rewards are also low.

**Example**

- First race £10 bet stake = £10.90. Total loss £10.90.
- Second race £20 bet stake = £21.80. Total loss £32.70.
- Third race £40 bet stake = £43.60. Total loss £76.30.
- Fourth race £80 bet stake = £87.20. Total loss £163.50.

In the fourth race the favourite wins at 1/2. Returns = £120.
Total loss = £43.50.
If the favourite had won at 2/1. Returns = £240.
Total winnings = £76.50.

However, there is no guarantee that the favourite would win by the fourth race. If your stake becomes too high, a bookmaker may refuse your bet. You may also run out of capital before a favourite wins.

During the last few minutes before a race, prices can change drastically. Instead of there being just one favourite, a situation can arise where there are joint or even co-favourites. Where you just back the favourite without specifying the name of the horse, your winnings will be greatly reduced if the race is won by a joint favourite or co-favourite. In a situation where there are co-favourites of four, your winnings would only amount to a quarter of what you had expected. Since the prices of the favourites are low, you are unlikely to recoup your outlay.

Some people apply the system to second favourites because their prices are higher. The problem here is that second favourites win fewer races than favourites, so the capital needed is greater.

With this system, you are also making no assessment of the runners. By properly considering the chances of each horse, you may discover that another horse is more likely to win the race.

## Betting on horses that have travelled a long distance to race

The logic of this is that a trainer would not travel several hundred miles if the horse did not stand a good chance of winning. The problem with this system is that there may be an equally good horse in the race that has only travelled a short distance. Horses do travel all over the world. British horses are taken to America and France. However, this does not mean that they are guaranteed to win.

### Betting on horses that have an advantage on the draw

With a lot of British racecourses, the draw can have an effect on the race. Horses starting in certain positions in the stalls have an advantage over others. By combining your assessment of horses with this knowledge, it is possible to select several horses that have a good chance of winning. Instead of backing the horses to win, bets of combination tricasts are placed.

A tricast is predicting which horses will finish first, second and third in the correct order. For a small outlay, the returns are potentially huge.

A particularly good time of the year to play this bet is in the summer months when the ground has dried out and the form is starting to show through. At this time of year it is much easier to assess the horses. You do not have to worry about the going and you have lots of previous races on which to make your judgement.

In the 1980s bookmakers started to lose a lot of money through this system. Many were also offering huge bonuses of around 20 per cent on correct tricasts, which increased their losses. They are now extremely cautious about accepting bets on combination tricasts, particularly where the stakes are large. In order to get your bet accepted, you may need to spread it around several bookmakers.

## Effect of the draw at British and Irish racecourses

- Ascot: no significant advantage
- Ayr: 6 furlongs in large field – middle numbers; 7 furlongs and over – low numbers
- Bath: sprints – low numbers
- Beverley: 5-furlong course – high numbers
- Brighton: sprints – low numbers
- Carlisle: high numbers; however low numbers are favoured when the going is soft

- Catterick: low numbers
- Chepstow: straight course – high numbers; round course – low numbers
- Chester: round course 7½ furlongs – low numbers
- Curragh: high numbers
- Doncaster: round course – no advantage; straight course – low numbers
- Dundalk: no advantage
- Edinburgh: 7 furlongs and 1 mile races – high numbers
- Epsom: up to 8½ furlongs – low numbers
- Fairyhouse: no advantage
- Folkestone: straight 6-furlong course – low numbers
- Galway: high numbers
- Goodwood: sprint races – high numbers
- Gowran Park: no advantage
- Hamilton Park: straight course – middle to high numbers
- Haydock Park: 6 furlongs to 1 mile – low numbers; if going soft on straight course – high numbers
- Kempton Park: round course – high numbers
- Killarney: no advantage
- Laytown: no advantage
- Leicester: straight course up to 1 mile – middle to high numbers (even more so on soft ground)
- Leopardstown: slight advantage to low number
- Lingfield Park: straight course – high numbers if the going is heavy, otherwise low numbers
- Newbury: no advantage
- Newcastle: no advantage
- Newmarket: no advantage
- Nottingham: straight course – high numbers; round course – low numbers
- Pontefract: sprints – low numbers
- Redcar: sprints – high numbers
- Ripon: straight course – low numbers; round course – high numbers
- Salisbury: if the going is soft – low numbers
- Sandown Park: 5-furlong course – high numbers when the going is soft
- Thirsk: straight course – high numbers; round course – low numbers
- Warwick: races up to 8 furlongs – high numbers (more marked when the going is soft)
- Windsor: sprints – high numbers; on soft ground – low numbers

- Wolverhampton: no advantage
- Yarmouth: straight course – high numbers; round course – low numbers
- York: soft ground – low numbers; over 7 furlongs – low numbers

# Syndicate betting

You may consider forming a betting syndicate. You need to find a number of people who all want to bet as part of a team. Each person contributes an agreed amount of capital and any winnings are shared between all the members.

There are several advantages. You do not have to play for high stakes. You have the opportunity to make a wider range of bets than your capital alone will allow. The work of assessing the horses can be shared between the members.

## How to organize a syndicate

Only take part in syndicates with people whom you know and trust. Find a number of people whom you see on a regular basis. Family, friends and work colleagues are the most likely choices.

Although a verbal agreement is legally binding it is worth taking the time to draw up a written agreement that can be relied on if there is a dispute. You may think it sounds like a lot of trouble to go to, but consider the situation that would arise if the syndicate won a great deal of money with, for example, an accumulator. Suppose that particular week you had forgotten to pay your contribution. Would you be entitled to a share of the winnings? Without a written agreement covering that eventuality you would have a lot of trouble proving your case. What would happen if someone had dropped out the week before and now insisted that they were still in the syndicate? How could you prove that they had left the syndicate? If you draw up a written agreement it can save on both the expense and the time taken for court proceedings.

## What to include in the agreement

You may think of other things to include but the main requirements are as follows:

* the date that the agreement starts
* when the agreement ends
* the full names and addresses of every member
* how much each person pays
* when the payments should be made
* what happens when someone wants to withdraw from the syndicate

Instead of having a continuous agreement it may be better to operate it for a number of weeks. At the end of that period you can assess if the agreement is working or if it needs to be amended in some way.

Ensure that all members sign and date the agreement, and that each person is given a copy. Make sure you have a contact number for all members in the event of something going wrong.

Insist that anyone wanting to withdraw from the agreement should do so in writing. Make sure you keep a copy of the letter in case of future disputes.

# 05 betting tips

**In this chapter you will learn:**

- **how bookmakers make a profit**
- **about setting a budget**
- **about making the best bet**
- **which bets to avoid.**

Winning at horse racing involves a lot more than simply selecting the best horses. Many factors have an influence on how profitable you will be. We have already seen how bookmakers make a profit. Around 17 per cent of the betting turnover is guaranteed to go to them regardless of the race result. Depending on where you bet, you may need to overcome taxation, which is between 5 and 20 per cent. In order to win at horse racing you need to find a way of betting that overcomes these factors and gives you a profit on your stakes.

## Be aware of the rules

When you place a bet make sure you fully understand the rules. Each year, a small fortune in winning bets is not claimed. This is often due to bettors misunderstanding the rules. Bets where the punter must write out a betting slip, as in Great Britain, are particularly prone to mistakes. A bet may illegible, incorrectly written or wrongly timed. Ask for a copy of the rules and take them home and study them.

As well as the betting rules, learn the rules that apply to horse racing. If you bet at a racecourse and there is a stewards' enquiry, there could be an amended result. While the enquiry is in progress, the bookmakers will often lay odds on the outcome. If you saw the incident, which led to the enquiry, and have a thorough knowledge of horse racing, you can use this to your advantage and bet on the outcome.

## Appreciate your chances of winning

Have a thorough understanding of the odds against winning. The prices offered by bookmakers are not the realistic chances that a horse has of winning. The bookmaker has adjusted the odds to allow him or herself to make a profit. If you learn how to calculate the profit on a book, you can judge whether or not it is worth having a bet.

## How bookmakers make a profit

The prices change constantly as more bets are placed. A big bet on a horse will result in its price being lowered. If horses are not attracting bets, their prices will be increased.

Bookmakers aim to make a profit on each race. On average the minimum profit on each race is around 17 per cent. For some books the profit may be slightly less and for others it will be much greater. To find out if you are getting value for money, you can calculate how much profit the bookmaker is taking. You may decide that it is not worthwhile betting because the bookmaker's profit is too high.

## Calculating the profit

1 Apply the following formula to each price:

$$\frac{100 \times b}{(a + b)}$$

a = the number on the left of the price
b = the number on the right of the price

2 Add together the amounts found in 1.
3 Deduct 100.

The balance is the percentage profit made by the bookmaker.

**Example**

A three-horse race may initially have the following prices:

A 1/2
B 2/1
C 5/1

**1** A $\frac{100 \times 2}{(1 + 2)} = 66.66$

B $\frac{100 \times 1}{(2 + 1)} = 33.33$

C $\frac{100 \times 1}{(5 + 1)} = 16.66$

**2** 66.66 + 33.33 + 16.66 = 116.65
**3** 116.65 – 100 = 16.65

Here the bookmaker is making 16.65 per cent profit. This is around the 17 per cent mark. Where the profit is greater than 17 per cent you are not getting good value for money. The lower the bookmaker's profit, the better it is for you.

Races with fewer runners give smaller profits for bookmakers and are consequently better for gamblers. This is because there are fewer runners on which the bookmaker can add his or her profit. Conversely, races with a large number of runners give bigger profits.

One of the reasons why it is so important to assess the prices of the horses yourself is that sometimes the bookmakers can get the odds wrong. If you can spot this, you are more likely to win. Two former betting shop managers realized that the odds offered by bookmakers for getting a hole-in-one in golfing championships was much higher than the actual chances. The true odds of a hole-in-one in major tournaments were around 2/1. Some bookmakers had not properly assessed the chances and were offering odds as high as 100/1. This represented a huge difference and was worthwhile betting on. The two men gave up work and travelled around the UK betting with small bookmakers on this event. Over the course of a year they staked £30,000 and won approximately £500,000. Once the bookmakers realized their error it was too late, although some did refuse to pay out.

It is unlikely to happen again with holes-in-one in golf as everyone is aware of that, but a situation could arise where the bookmaker has failed to make a proper assessment of all the odds. By using the formulae for assessing probability and calculating odds, you can check if a bookmaker is getting it right.

## Keep records of your gambling

Try to keep accurate records of your betting. Also, write down the reasons why you win or lose. Analyse your results periodically. By keeping records you will be in a much better position to assess your betting strategy and to make changes if it is not effective.

## Illegal gambling

If you bet legally you can ensure that you are fairly treated. However, by betting illegally you have no guarantee. People are usually tempted to bet illegally to avoid paying tax. There are several problems with illegal bookmakers. They may take your money and run, or simply refuse to pay you. Since gambling debts are not recoverable through the courts, there is nothing you can do about it.

Alternatively the illegal bookmaker may offer you credit. If your bets lose, your credit is increased. Gradually your debts accumulate. Then the bookmaker turns nasty, wants his or her money back and starts charging an extortionate amount of interest on the balance that you owe. The bookmaker cannot get his or her money through legal action, so may go to any lengths to get you to pay up.

## Set a budget

Calculate your disposable income by deducting your living expenses from your income. Then decide how much of your disposable income you can comfortably afford to lose. The amount you have calculated is your budget for gambling.

Be sure to stick to your budget. Never be tempted to make additional bets from, for example, your rent money. If you keep to your budget you can gamble with the knowledge that no matter how much you lose, you will not go bankrupt.

Even if your budget is small, you can still enjoy betting on horse racing. The minimum stakes are low. In a betting shop, you can place a bet for as little as 20p. People betting low stakes make up the majority of a betting shop's customers. Another way to make your money go further is from a betting syndicate with other gamblers. This enables you to pool your knowledge with the other members of the syndicate and to place a greater range of bets than you could normally afford.

When you go out gambling take only your stake money and enough for your expenses (fare home, drinks, meals, etc.). Leave all chequebooks and cash cards at home. If you cannot get your hands on more money, you cannot spend it. Do not be tempted to borrow money from friends. Decline all offers of credit. If you run out of money, either go home or just watch the racing.

If you do not want to carry large amounts of cash, open a separate bank account for your gambling money and take with you only the chequebook and cards relating to that account when you gamble. By having a sensible approach to gambling you can ensure that you do not lose more than you can afford.

Also take extra care if you have a big win. It is not necessary to take all your winnings in cash. Accepting a cheque from the bookmaker for all or part of the winnings is much safer than carrying around large amounts of cash, which can easily be stolen from you.

When you have a big win do not be tempted to start placing large bets. It is very tempting as soon as you collect your winnings to place a large bet on the next race. If you have not properly assessed the race, you are simply relying on luck alone. It is best to stick to your tried and tested methods, and to bet only when you are certain that you have a good chance of winning.

## Take account of all costs

As well as the cost of your bets, there will be additional expenses that you need to include.

### Betting tax and other deductions

In most countries there is some sort of taxation applied to horse racing. The horse racing industry, racetracks and horse racing associations also often take a cut of betting turnover. The deductions applied to horse racing vary around the world between zero and as much as 24 per cent. Tote betting commonly has the biggest deductions. In the USA deductions vary from 15 to 25 per cent for single bets and 19 to 35 per cent for multiple bets. Irish betting shops charge a 5 per cent tax and British betting shops charge nothing. Offshore betting operators offer tax-free betting, however they make a service charge, which is typically 3 per cent. There is tax-free betting with bookmakers at British and Irish racecourses. If you are betting large stakes and intend making several bets, it may be more profitable to attend the race meeting rather than bet in a betting shop.

If you bet with an on-course bookmaker and are betting each-way, pay particular attention to how many places and what fraction of the odds they are offering as some offer better deals than others. The bookmakers also offer additional bets, like betting on the outcome of a photo finish or stewards' enquiry so it is worth getting a good view of the race. If you see an incident happen at close quarters you can make yourself some extra money by betting on it.

The bookmakers on the course are independent so you will find that they will all be offering slightly different prices. Each bookmaker has his or her own book to balance, so the prices offered will depend on what bets he or she has personally taken. It is worthwhile taking your time to shop around for the best price for your selection. However, do not take too long to decide where to bet as the prices can quickly change.

## Admission charges

Although British and Irish racecourses offer tax-free betting, this can often be offset by admission fees and travelling costs. The admission charges vary, increasing when prestigious meetings are held. These costs can be reduced by joining a racing club or by organizing group outings to gain discounts on admission and to reduce travelling costs.

## Sporting newspapers

A good quality racing newspaper is essential from which to glean all the up-to-date racing news. Using library and betting shop copies can eliminate this cost. An enormous amount of information also appears on the Internet, which is ideal for the latest news.

## Refreshments

If you go to a race meeting, taking a picnic is part of the social occasion and is much cheaper than eating in a restaurant. Avoid drinking alcohol as it impairs your judgement and encourages you to bet more recklessly.

## Phone calls

Many bookmakers offer facilities for customers to bet over the telephone. You will need to take into account the cost of the calls, which can be a considerable expense over a period of time. Try shopping around, as some bookmakers offer free calls, which can save you a lot of money.

Telephone results and tipsters' services are charged at a premium rate, so can be costly. Although they are convenient to use, it is much cheaper to check results and get tips from other sources, such as newspapers, teletext and the radio.

## Your time

Your time can be one of the costliest parts of gambling. To be profitable you will often have to devote an enormous amount of time to assessing runners. Each horse, jockey and trainer's performance needs to be looked at in detail. A horse's preference for different ground also needs to be taken into consideration. Up-to-date records are essential. Yesterday's results can completely change the picture. Gathering all this information takes time. So, too, does analysing it.

You can cut down on the amount of time needed by forming a syndicate. The task of assessing the runners can then be divided between the members (see page 68).

## Be selective

You do not have to bet on every race. It pays to be selective; this way your money will last longer. Carefully choose the races that you bet on. Not every race offers good betting opportunities. Some races are simply too competitive, making it extremely hard to select the winner. If a race is too competitive, ignore it. Your assessment of the horses may only find a few bets each week that are worth making. By only betting on horses that have a realistic chance of winning you will increase your profits. Any new strategy should be tested initially with low stakes. It can be costly if the stakes are high and the strategy is not effective. If you have a losing streak, stop betting and reassess your strategy.

## Take your time

Do not wait until the day of the race to assess the runners. You can do this in advance as the race cards are published ahead of time. Take your time and give careful consideration to your selections. This gives you time to assess the horses competing in forthcoming races.

## Maximize returns

It is not just necessary to identify winners. To gain as big a profit as possible you need to identify high-priced winners. Remember the prices on offer reflect the amount of money bet on them. They are not the chances that a horse has of winning. In the Grand National four horses have won at odds of 100/1. A high-priced winner is clearly more profitable than one at a low price.

Many people assume that if they are backing a high-priced horse, they should reduce their stakes. This is not true. If your selection has a high price, back it at your usual stake level.

## Be realistic

Do not expect to win on every race. Do not bet your entire stake on one horse. A spread of bets is less risky.

If you start losing do not be tempted to make big bets to recoup your losses.

## How bookmakers try to make you spend more money

Betting shops are in business to make a profit. They want you to spend as much time as possible on their premises. To keep you there they try to make the shops as comfortable as possible. Refreshments are usually available so that you need not leave if you are hungry or thirsty.

There is always something for you to bet on. Greyhound racing is interspersed with the horse racing to get you to bet as much as possible. It also starts earlier than the horse racing and finishes later to try to encourage you to bet both while you put on your bets before the horse racing starts and when you are collecting any winnings at the end of the horse racing. Sports betting is also heavily advertised. Many sporting events are also televized in the shops to encourage you to stay and bet.

The staff are trained to tempt you to switch to bets that are more profitable for the bookmaker. Each day there are special offer bets advertised with bonuses and consolations. They are always the type of bets that give the bookmakers the biggest profits. Often example bets are shown written on the white boards. Again they are the bets that are highly profitable for the bookmaker. On major race days, vouchers are often given away for free bets that can be used the following week. This is to ensure that you come back.

The betting slips for the most profitable bets are colourful and prominently displayed. Instructions for completing the slip are printed on them. However, if you want to make a bet that is more profitable for you, it has to be written on a blank slip. No instructions are supplied.

Competitions that are usually free to enter are often run. The most common type is for the customer to select one horse each day. The customer who has theoretically won the most money by the end of the week wins a prize. This ensures that you visit the betting shop every day. The bookmaker knows that as soon as you are on the premises you are likely to have a bet.

Everything is designed with profit in mind, even the way the newspapers are displayed. The greyhound cards are arranged nearest the counter where the bets are placed. This ensures that you do not have too far to run when the hare is running (a race is about to start). The main meetings of the day are usually placed opposite the screens. This means you can look at the prices and, when you turn around, the race card for the meeting is directly opposite you.

The tipsters' boxes on the racing newspapers are often highlighted. These give the top tips for each daily newspaper. They are usually for short-priced favourites. The bookmakers want the customers to bet on these horses. They know that statistically it is highly unlikely that the favourite will win every race. Favourites lose around 60 per cent of their races. Even on the races they do win, their prices will be small; so, too, will the payouts. Conversely the bookmaker's profits will be high.

Due to the low prices of the favourites, customers are also more likely to bet on them to win rather than each-way. This is also to the bookmaker's advantage, as win bets are more profitable than each-way bets.

Betting shops also allow customers to collect their winnings before the weigh-in. This is to ensure that you have your money in time to place a bet on the next race. Even if there is an amended result, the disadvantage to the bookmaker is far outweighed by the speed at which the money is re-bet.

## Ground

A good time to bet is when the ground has dried out towards the end of the flat season. The form is also more established which means you have more information about the current season on which to base your selections. You need to bear in mind that some grounds dry out in an irregular way which could give horses on the dryer ground an advantage.

## Type of race

The type of race will have an influence on whether or not it is worthwhile making a bet. Amateur, apprentice, ladies' and novice races are too unpredictable and best avoided. The top races are too competitive as they attract the best horses. Races where there is a range of runners and experience are better.

With national hunt there is always the danger that your selection could fall or refuse to jump. Trotting races also have their danger. Horses get disqualified if they do not trot and are easily boxed in. This makes flat racing the best choice.

## Betting on handicap races

Since handicap races are designed to give all horses an equal chance, they are ideal for backing high-priced runners. All the runners have a chance of winning which means a high-priced runner also stands a good chance. Here the best value bet is each-way. Even if your selection fails to win but is placed you will still get a decent return. If there are more than 16 runners, then you will be paid even if your horse comes in fourth. You do not just have to stick to one selection. With four places to contend, you can select four horses, giving yourself four times as many chances of winning. This can be demonstrated as follows.

**Example**

Suppose you bet £8 win on a horse at 3/1, your returns would be £32. If your selection comes second, third or fourth, you lose.

If instead you bet each-way on four horses at fairly high prices, for example 25/1. You now have four chances of winning. The stake is the same £8. The best outcome is that one horse will win and the other three are placed. This would give returns of £110. If one horse wins and two are placed, the returns are £95.50. If only one horse is placed the returns are £7.25. This means that the stake is almost recovered.

With handicaps the statistics point to the fact that around 48 per cent of winners of flat races are in the top four in the weights and 62 per cent of winners are in the top six in the weights.

However, there are some races where the top weights do not fare well. In the Grand National, for example, horses from the top end of the handicap tend to do poorly.

## Number of runners

Too many runners can make the selection of a winner very difficult. The Grand National is great fun to watch, but not to bet on. There are far too many runners and the difficulty of the fences means that only a minority of the horses finish. Too many incidents during the race make successful betting very hard.

## Backing favourites

The problem with backing favourites is that only around 40 per cent of favourites win. Favourites also have the lowest price so it means that any returns are not significant. There is also little value in betting each-way due to the low price.

## Take the best price

If you have done your homework, you will know what a good price is for your horse. If you are betting in a betting shop, always take a price on your selection, particularly if you are betting on fancied horses. Just before the off, the betting is frantic. This can result in the prices of the fancied horses being hugely reduced between the last show and when the starting price is returned.

At the racecourse shop around. Each bookmaker offers individual odds. Try to get yourself the best deal possible. Do not be afraid to negotiate a better price or terms. You may find that a bookmaker will give a little extra rather than let his competitors have your business.

One way to get a better price is to quote the true odds based on the way the prices have been calculated. The standard range of prices that you see on offer has been derived from a fraction of 100 and rounded down. A price of 6/1 has been calculated from the fraction of 100/16 which works out as 6¼ /1. This is then rounded down to 6/1. You can try to get a better price from the bookmaker by calling out '50 to 8 Dobbin'. By doing this you increase your returns by £2. The following table gives the fractions for the standard prices and the percentage increase on returns.

| Standard price | As a fraction of 100 | Odds to one | % increase on returns |
|---|---|---|---|
| 3/1 | 100/33 | $3\frac{1}{3} - 1$ | 1 |
| 6/1 | 100/16 | $6\frac{1}{4} - 1$ | 4 |
| 7/1 | 100/14 | $7\frac{1}{7} - 1$ | 2 |
| 8/1 | 100/12 | $8\frac{1}{3} - 1$ | 4 |
| 12/1 | 100/8 | $12\frac{1}{2} - 1$ | 4 |
| 14/1 | 100/7 | $14\frac{2}{7} - 1$ | 2 |
| 16/1 | 100/6 | $16\frac{2}{3} - 1$ | 4 |
| 33/1 | 100/3 | $33\frac{1}{3} - 1$ | 1 |

If you are betting on a high-priced horse, you may be able to negotiate a bigger price. As the off time for the race gets nearer, there is often a great deal of betting on the lower-priced horses whose prices can be drastically reduced. The prices of the other horses should lengthen but often they tend to get forgotten as the bookmaker is focusing all his or her attention on the fancied horses. If you want to bet on a higher-priced horse and its price has not been lengthened, try to negotiate a bigger price.

## Making the best bet

The type of bet you make can influence how much money you win. Some bets are more profitable for the punter than others. Some bets are so unprofitable for the punter that they are simply not worth making. By understanding which bets give the best value, a shrewd gambler can drastically reduce the bookmaker's advantage.

A British study by Nottingham University that compared the betting patterns of men and women found that women won more than men. The reasons for this were that women did not take ridiculous risks. Men were more reckless, often betting on long shots. Instead of betting to win, women were more likely to bet each-way, which is a more profitable bet.

**The profitability of bets**

| Type of bet | Betting shop's advantage (%) |
|---|---|
| Ante-post | 0 |
| Each-way singles at board price | 4 |
| Each-way singles at starting price | 5 |
| Win singles at board price | 6 |
| Win singles at starting price | 8 |
| Each-way doubles | 8 |
| Win doubles | 10 |
| Forecast singles | 12 |
| Each-way multiple bets | 18 |
| Win multiple bets | 23 |
| Forecast doubles | 40 |

Ante-post bets give you the best value for money. Bookmakers consider themselves fortunate if they break even on these bets. Many people are put off betting ante-post because of the risk of losing their stake if a horse is withdrawn. However, this risk is far outweighed by the more favourable odds that are offered.

The larger ante-post bets are often placed by people who have received information. Even though you may not be in a position to glean that information, it is possible to guess it by monitoring price changes. A large drop in price on a horse can be an indication that there has been a big bet on it.

## Betting each-way

One of the most profitable bets is an each-way single. These give bookmakers a 4 per cent profit. Consider a result where the favourite wins at 2/1 and a horse at 25/1 comes third. A £1 bet on the winner would give a net profit of £1.73, while a £1 each-way bet on the third horse gives a net profit of £3.46 (calculated at 1/5 odds).

Instead of trying to select the winner, it can be more profitable to find which horses will be placed. You also have the added bonus that your selection may just win the race. If your 25/1 horse wins the returns will be £29.12.

Different strategies require different bets. If you are backing a high-priced runner, it makes sense to back it each-way as you will still get a decent return if it is placed.

**Place odds for each-way bets**

The number of places and the fraction of odds paid for the place bet are determined by the number of runners and the type of race:

| Number of runners | Type of race | Number of places | Fraction of win odds |
|---|---|---|---|
| 16 or more | handicap | 4 | 1/4 |
| 12 to 15 | handicap | 3 | 1/4 |
| 8 to 15 | not applicable | 3 | 1/5 |
| 5 to 7 | not applicable | 2 | 1/4 |
| 4 or less | not applicable | 1 (win only) | both bets win |

# Bets to avoid

Bets to avoid making are all multiple bets like yankees, canadians, heinz and lucky 15. They give bookmakers the biggest profits. The reason for this is that if one horse loses, instead of losing just one bet, you lose several.

Consider a yankee. It is 11 bets in six doubles, four trebles and a fourfold. If you bet on horses A, B, C and D, then your bets are as follows:

- doubles: AB, AC, AD, BC, BD and CD
- trebles: ABC, ABD, ACD and BCD
- fourfold: ABCD

If horse A loses, you have automatically lost seven bets. All you are left with are four bets BC, BD, CD and BCD. If horse B also loses, you have only one bet left – CD.

Alternatively, make a bet like a super heinz and you lose a massive 63 bets if one of your horses loses. This is the reason why multiple bets are so heavily advertised by the betting shops. They are made to look attractive because bonuses are often added if all of your selections win. However these bonuses rarely get paid because the odds of picking out several winners all on the same day and combining them in one bet are very slim. Even if you do achieve this, the small print of the rules often stipulates that bonuses are paid at starting price odds and not at the prices that you may have taken. Some betting shops also substitute non-runners for the favourite. Again this gives them a bigger profit. Suppose you play a multiple bet that contains doubles. If you have one winner and a non-runner you would be paid the equivalent of a win single. By putting the favourite in the place of the non-runner, the bookmaker has the advantage that the favourite may lose. Favourites lose around 60 per cent of their races, so the bookmaker has a 60 per cent advantage of your bet losing. Even if the favourite wins, its price will be low so the bookmaker will not have to pay out very much.

## Placing large bets

If you are unable to go to a racecourse and want to place a large bet, you need to be particularly careful. Betting shops are notorious for refusing to accept bets at the current advertised odds and, instead, offer you a lower price. They use this tactic as a means of increasing their profits.

Consider what happens if you want to bet £1,000 on a horse whose current price is 7/1. You calculate that if you pay the tax, your returns will be £8,000.

Your bet will be immediately passed to the shop manager who will phone head office. The betting chain employs representatives who place bets for them with bookmakers at the racecourse. The head office will contact their representative and ask what the best price is for the horse you want to back. Suppose 7/1 is the best price on offer.

You may be told that your bet will be accepted but only at odds of 6/1. Now, instead of winning £8,000, you will only get £7,000. You have effectively lost £1,000. You are not in a position to bargain, since if you go to another shop, the price may be further reduced. You have to decide whether or not you still want to place the bet.

If you agree to accept the reduced odds of 6/1, the on-course representative will be instructed to place £875 on the horse. He or she will get odds of 7/1 giving him or her returns of £7,000 if the horse wins. The representative has also managed to make a profit of £125 on the bet as he or she was able to take advantage of better odds than you. For the price of a phone call the betting shop has cut your winnings by £1,000 and made itself a 12½ per cent profit on your stake.

To overcome the problem of being offered reduced odds, you need to spread your bets around different shops. It is best to bet with different chains of shops as nearby shops of the same chain may contact one another if they are suspicious about your bet because it is just under the limit for hedging. By placing small bets in several shops you will be able to take the advertised odds.

The maximum amount that you can bet will vary with different betting shops. With the big chains bets up to £200 will usually be accepted without any problems. With small chains, bets under £50 or with returns of less than £1,000 will usually be accepted. On major race days like the Cheltenham meeting and the Grand National meeting, the limits are usually doubled so you can get away with placing larger bets.

Betting shops keep their limits for large bets confidential, but it is fairly easy to discover them with a little stealth. Simply write out a large bet on a horse that has the same price as the one you want to bet on. Hand it to the cashier and pretend to be looking for your wallet. If the bet is passed to the manager and he reaches for the phone, you know you have exceeded the limit. If nothing happens, you know you can safely bet on your selection. Whatever the outcome, ask for your slip to be returned as you cannot find your wallet. You can then write out a slip for your selection, safe in the knowledge that you will not be offered a reduced price.

## Big winners

Bookmakers are in the business of making a profit. If you are continually winning large amounts, you are reducing their profit. For this reason they try to discourage people that are winning a lot. They achieve this by monitoring people who win on a regular basis. All large wins in betting shops are recorded, typically wins of £500 or over are noted, although smaller wins may be noted if you win regularly. After several big wins a situation will arise when all your bets will be monitored. Every single bet that you place will be recorded. Your total stakes will be compared to your total winnings. The bookmaker will then take a decision based on your results. If he or she thinks you are winning too much, you may suddenly find that your bets are refused or have a limit placed on them.

If this happens to you, it is useless trying to argue your case. You should simply place your bets with an alternative chain. However, you can guard against this happening by betting in several different shops. If you have several big wins, change to another shop.

## Steamers

The price that each horse attains in the betting is determined by the amount of money that has been bet on it. A horse that has the most money bet on it will have the lowest price and will be the favourite. A horse may first appear in the betting as an outsider. If lots of large bets are placed on the horse to win, its price will be drastically reduced. Often gamblers making large bets have information that the horse has a good chance of winning. In some cases a horse may be backed down from an outsider to the favourite. Horses whose prices drop in this manner are called steamers.

Betting on steamers involves keeping a close eye on the betting market. Bets are made on outsiders whose prices are quickly falling. You need to spot the steamers as early as possible to achieve the best possible price before it drops too low.

This is where going to a race meeting can make a big difference. You have the advantage of seeing the changes in betting as they take place. In the first 15 minutes of betting the prices can change a lot as the market is formed. In a betting shop you miss out on all this action, as the prices are transmitted much later. You can still find the steamers, but at the racecourse you can spot them earlier and take advantage of a better price.

## Collecting winnings

Take advantage of the early payout of winnings by betting shops. Try to collect your winnings as soon as possible. Sometimes it can be several minutes after a race before a stewards' enquiry or objection is announced, at which point the betting shops will stop paying out. If you manage to collect your winnings before this announcement, you will not have to return them if the result is amended.

Do not throw away losing betting slips until the race has weighed in. The result of a race is not official until the weigh-in is announced. A stewards' enquiry or objection may be called before the weigh-in. Even if your horse was last past the post, there is still a chance that you could have your stake refunded. The entire race may be voided. If you have thrown away your slip you then need to search on the floor, which is likely to be covered in discarded slips. Also there is always the chance that someone else may find your slip before you, and collect on it.

# 06 checking the results and calculating your winnings

**In this chapter you will learn:**

- how to check the results
- how to calculate your winnings
- how to solve disputes with bookmakers
- how to use a ready reckoner.

## Checking the results

Horse racing results are available in many places, including the betting shop, newspapers, teletext, the internet, television (if the racing is broadcast), radio and from the telephone racing lines.

Always double-check results the following morning in a good-quality racing newspaper. Some of the daily tabloid newspapers and text services are notorious for printing the wrong results. If there are printing errors in the quality racing newspapers these are always communicated to the betting shops.

When you check the results be sure to look out for any factors that may affect the settlement of your bet. These include non-runners, dead-heats and rule 4 deductions. If betting on unnamed favourites, check for joint or co-favourites. For each-way bets note the number of runners that actually ran and whether or not the race was a handicap. This allows you to work out the place odds that apply.

Check that your selection was a runner. If it did not run you may be entitled to a refund.

## Disputes with bookmakers

Do not be afraid to query a bet if you think it has been incorrectly settled. Ask the settler to explain his or her calculations. In a betting shop, query the amount with the manager. Should this fail to bring a solution, the next step is to try the head office of the company. If the bookmaker is a member of the Independent Betting Arbitration Service, you can apply to IBAS for a resolution. The address is on page 105.

## Calculating your winnings

It is vitally important that you know how to calculate the winnings on your bets. Settlers may have a couple of thousand bets to deal with on a daily basis. Each bet is calculated literally in seconds. Mistakes do occur, so always check your payouts.

### Where the stake fits the price

Most of the calculations to settle bets will involve initially working out the returns to a £1 stake on each price. However, if a win single is being calculated and the stake fits the price it may often be easier to settle.

As we have seen the prices are comprised of two numbers: the number on the left is the amount that will be won if the amount on the right is staked. The stake is also returned.

If the stake is the same as the number on the right of the price then the bet is very easy to settle. Also if the stake is a multiple of the number on the right, the bet can be easily settled with the minimum of arithmetic.

**Example 1**

£1 win @ 7/1.
The stake is £1 which is the same as the number on the right of the price. The winnings are therefore the amount on the left of the price which is £7. The stake is also refunded, so the total returns are 7 + 1 = £8.

**Example 2**

£4 win @ 9/2.
The stake is £4. This is double the amount on the right of the price. The winnings will therefore be double the amount on the left of the price (2 × 9 = 18). The stake is also refunded, so the total returns are 18 + 4 = £22.

**Example 3**

£4 win @ 13/8.
The stake is £4. This is half the number on the right of the price, so the winnings will be half the amount on the left of the price, (13/2 = £6.50). The stake is also refunded, therefore the total returns are 6.5 + 4 = £10.50.

# Finding the returns to a one-unit stake

This method of settling allows you to work out the returns to any stake unit. Once you know what the returns are to a one-unit stake, you can simply multiply your stake by that amount to find your winnings.

## Win bets

There are two ways to find the returns to a £1 stake.

**Method 1**

- Add together the left and right numbers of the price.
- Divide by the right number of the price.

**Method 2**

- Divide the left number by the right number.
- Add 1.

**Examples**

Finding the £1 returns for each of the following prices using Method 1.

8/11 $\frac{8+11}{11} = \frac{19}{11} = 1.7272$

11/8 $\frac{11+8}{8} = \frac{19}{8} = 2.375$

7/2 $\frac{7+2}{2} = \frac{9}{2} = 4.5$

9/4 $\frac{9+4}{4} = \frac{13}{4} = 3.25$

## Settling win singles

1 Find the returns to a £1 stake on the price.
2 Multiply by the stake.

**Example 1**

Using Method 1

£5 win @ 7/4. Stake = £5.00

1) $\frac{7+4}{4} = 2.75$

2) $2.75 \times 5 = 13.75$
Returns = £13.75

Using Method 2

1) $\frac{7}{4} = 1.75$

$1.75 + 1 = 2.75$

2) $2.75 \times 5 = 13.75$
Returns = £13.75

**Example 2**

£20 win @ 13/8. Stake = £20.00

1) $13 + 8 = 21$

$$\frac{21}{8} = 2.625$$

2) $2.625 \times 20 = 52.50$
Returns = £52.50

# Each-way singles

Each-way bets are two bets. One bet is for the selection to win, the other is for the selection to be placed. The place part of the bet is calculated at a fraction of the win price. For horse racing the fractions are 1/4 and 1/5.

The number of runners and whether or not the race is a handicap determines at what fraction the place part of the bet is calculated as follows:

- 1 to 4 runners – win only
- 5 to 7 runners – 1/4 odds
- 8 or more runners – 1/5 odds

## Handicap races

- 12 to 15 runners – 1/4 odds
- 16 or more runners – 1/4 odds

## All up to win

All up to win is an expression used where an each-way bet has been put on a race with four runners or fewer. It is not possible to bet each-way on these races so the place stakes are put on to win.

**Example**

Ascot 2.30
Selection A
£5.00 each-way
Stake = £10.00

If there were four or fewer runners in the race, then the bet would be settled as £10 win selection A.

For each-way multiple bets, the place and win parts need to be calculated separately. Here the £1 return on the place part of the bet is the same as the win bet. Therefore calculate the £1 returns on the win part of the bet and use the same amount for the place part of the bet in all further calculations.

## Each-way winners

If an each-way bet has been placed on a winner, there is a quick method for calculating the returns. This can only be used for each-way singles, it does not work for multiples.

### Method

1 Find the returns for a £1 stake on the winning price.
2 Deduct 1.
3 Multiply by 1.25 for 1/4 odds, or by 1.2 for 1/5 odds.
4 Add 2.
5 Multiply by the unit stake.

**Example 1**

£2 each-way winner @ 5/2 (1/5 odds). Tax paid. Stake = £4.36

1) £1 @ 5/2 = 3.5
2) 3.5 – 1 = 2.5
3) 2.5 × 1.2 (1/5 odds) = 3
4) 3 + 2 = 5
5) 5 × 2 = 10

Returns = £10.00

**Example 2**

£5 each-way winner @ 7/4 (1/4 odds). Stake = £10.00

1) £1 @ 7/4 = 2.75
2) 2.75 – 1 = 1.75
3) 1.75 × 1.25 (1/4 odds) = 2.1875
4) 2.1875 + 2 = 4.1875
5) 4.1875 × 5 = 20.9375

Returns = £20.94

# Non-runners in doubles

There is often a lot confusion over the settling of doubles where one selection is a non-runner. A double is a bet on two selections if the first selection wins, the returns are bet on the second selection. If the first selection is a non-runner, the returns from the first selection are the original stake, so the original stake goes onto the second selection.

**Example**

£1 win double AB. A is a non-runner. B is a winner at 2/1.

£1 is bet on selection A; as it is a winner the stake is refunded. Returns = £1.

These returns go on to the second selection. £1 @ 2/1 = £3. Total returns = £3.

# Using a ready reckoner

Using a ready reckoner is an easy way of calculating the winnings on your bets. The prices are listed numerically with the lowest price first. There are four columns in each table; the first column gives the stake, the second the win returns, the third the place returns at 1/5 odds, and the fourth the place returns at 1/4 odds.

To settle bets:

1 Find the price of each selection in the tables.
2 Find the stake and read across the amount in the appropriate column. For some stakes not shown it may be necessary to add together the amounts in different columns. For example, the stake for £15 is not given, therefore it would be necessary to look up the stakes for £10 and £5 and add them together.

**Example 1**

£5 win @ 7/4. Stake = £5.45
Find the table for 7/4.
Find the stake, in this case £5, and read off the amount in the win column = £13.75.
Returns = £13.75

**Example 2**

Winner £3 each-way @ 13/2 (1/4 odds). Stake = £6.00
Find the table for 13/2.
Find £3 and read off the amount in the win column = £22.50
Read off the amount for 1/4 odds = £7.87
Add both returns 22.50 + 7.87 = 30.375.
Returns = £30.38

**Example 3**

£10 win double 11/8 and 8/13. Stake = £10.90
Find the table for 11/8.
Find the stake of £10 and read off the amount in the win column = 23.75.
As the bet is a double, all the returns from the first selection go onto the second selection.
Find the table for 8/13. The stake is £23.75. As this stake is not in the table, look up the amount for £10 and double it.
Find the amounts for £3, 50p, 20p and 5p.
Total all the individual amounts.
32.30 + 4.84 + 0.80 + 0.32 + 0.08 = 38.34
Returns = £38.34

# appendix 1

## Ready Reckoner

| Price Stake | 2/7 Win | 2/7 1/5 odds | 2/7 1/4 odds | 1/3 Win | 1/3 1/5 odds | 1/3 1/4 odds | 4/11 Win | 4/11 1/5 odds | 4/11 1/4 odds | 2/5 Win | 2/5 1/5 odds | 2/5 1/4 odds | Price Stake |
|---|---|---|---|---|---|---|---|---|---|---|---|---|---|
| 5p | 0.06 | 0.05 | 0.05 | 0.06 | 0.10 | 0.05 | 0.06 | 0.05 | 0.05 | 0.07 | 0.05 | 0.05 | 5p |
| 10p | 0.12 | 0.10 | 0.10 | 0.13 | 0.10 | 0.10 | 0.13 | 0.10 | 0.10 | 0.14 | 0.10 | 0.11 | 10p |
| 20p | 0.25 | 0.21 | 0.21 | 0.26 | 0.21 | 0.21 | 0.27 | 0.21 | 0.21 | 0.28 | 0.21 | 0.22 | 20p |
| 50p | 0.64 | 0.54 | 0.53 | 0.66 | 0.53 | 0.54 | 0.68 | 0.53 | 0.54 | 0.70 | 0.54 | 0.55 | 50p |
| £1 | 1.28 | 1.05 | 1.07 | 1.33 | 1.06 | 1.08 | 1.36 | 1.07 | 1.09 | 1.40 | 1.08 | 1.10 | £1 |
| £2 | 2.56 | 2.11 | 2.14 | 2.66 | 2.13 | 2.16 | 2.72 | 2.14 | 2.18 | 2.80 | 2.16 | 2.20 | £2 |
| £3 | 3.85 | 3.17 | 3.21 | 4.00 | 3.19 | 3.25 | 4.09 | 3.21 | 3.27 | 4.20 | 3.24 | 3.30 | £3 |
| £4 | 5.14 | 4.22 | 4.28 | 5.33 | 4.26 | 4.33 | 5.45 | 4.29 | 4.36 | 5.60 | 4.32 | 4.40 | £4 |
| £5 | 6.42 | 5.28 | 5.35 | 6.66 | 5.33 | 5.41 | 6.81 | 5.36 | 5.45 | 7.00 | 5.40 | 5.50 | £5 |
| £6 | 7.71 | 6.34 | 6.42 | 8.00 | 6.40 | 6.50 | 8.18 | 6.43 | 6.54 | 8.40 | 6.48 | 6.60 | £6 |
| £7 | 9.00 | 7.40 | 7.50 | 9.33 | 7.46 | 7.58 | 9.54 | 7.50 | 7.63 | 9.80 | 7.56 | 7.70 | £7 |
| £8 | 10.28 | 8.45 | 8.57 | 10.66 | 8.53 | 8.66 | 10.90 | 8.58 | 8.72 | 11.20 | 8.64 | 8.80 | £8 |
| £9 | 11.57 | 9.51 | 9.64 | 12.00 | 9.60 | 9.75 | 12.27 | 9.65 | 9.81 | 12.60 | 9.72 | 9.90 | £9 |
| £10 | 12.85 | 10.57 | 10.71 | 13.33 | 10.66 | 10.83 | 13.63 | 10.72 | 10.90 | 14.00 | 10.80 | 11.00 | £10 |

| Price Stake | 4/9 Win | 4/9 1/5 odds | 4/9 1/4 odds | 40/85 Win | 40/85 1/5 odds | 40/85 1/4 odds | 1/2 Win | 1/2 1/5 odds | 1/2 1/4 odds | 8/15 Win | 8/15 1/5 odds | 8/15 1/4 odds | Price Stake |
|---|---|---|---|---|---|---|---|---|---|---|---|---|---|
| 5p | 0.07 | 0.10 | 0.11 | 0.07 | 0.05 | 0.05 | 0.07 | 0.05 | 0.05 | 0.07 | 0.05 | 0.05 | 5p |
| 10p | 0.14 | 0.10 | 0.11 | 0.14 | 0.10 | 0.11 | 0.15 | 0.11 | 0.11 | 0.15 | 0.11 | 0.11 | 10p |
| 20p | 0.28 | 0.21 | 0.22 | 0.29 | 0.21 | 0.22 | 0.30 | 0.22 | 0.22 | 0.30 | 0.22 | 0.22 | 20p |
| 50p | 0.72 | 0.54 | 0.55 | 0.73 | 0.54 | 0.55 | 0.75 | 0.55 | 0.56 | 0.76 | 0.55 | 0.56 | 50p |
| £1 | 1.44 | 1.08 | 1.11 | 1.47 | 1.09 | 1.11 | 1.50 | 1.10 | 1.12 | 1.53 | 1.10 | 1.13 | £1 |
| £2 | 2.88 | 2.17 | 2.22 | 2.94 | 2.18 | 2.23 | 3.00 | 2.20 | 2.25 | 3.06 | 2.21 | 2.26 | £2 |
| £3 | 4.33 | 3.26 | 3.33 | 4.41 | 3.28 | 3.35 | 4.50 | 3.30 | 3.37 | 4.60 | 3.31 | 3.40 | £3 |
| £4 | 5.77 | 4.35 | 4.44 | 5.88 | 4.37 | 4.47 | 6.00 | 4.40 | 5.06 | 6.13 | 4.42 | 4.53 | £4 |
| £5 | 7.22 | 5.44 | 5.55 | 7.35 | 5.47 | 5.58 | 7.50 | 5.50 | 5.62 | 7.66 | 5.53 | 5.66 | £5 |
| £6 | 8.66 | 6.53 | 6.66 | 8.82 | 6.56 | 6.70 | 9.00 | 6.60 | 6.75 | 9.20 | 6.64 | 6.80 | £6 |
| £7 | 10.11 | 7.62 | 7.77 | 10.29 | 7.65 | 7.82 | 10.50 | 7.70 | 7.87 | 10.73 | 7.74 | 7.93 | £7 |
| £8 | 11.55 | 8.71 | 8.88 | 11.76 | 8.75 | 8.94 | 12.00 | 8.80 | 9.00 | 12.26 | 8.85 | 9.06 | £8 |
| £9 | 13.00 | 9.79 | 10.00 | 13.23 | 9.84 | 10.05 | 13.50 | 9.90 | 10.12 | 13.80 | 9.96 | 10.20 | £9 |
| £10 | 14.44 | 10.88 | 11.11 | 14.70 | 10.94 | 11.17 | 15.00 | 11.00 | 11.25 | 15.33 | 11.06 | 11.33 | £10 |

| Price | 4/7 | | | 8/13 | | | 4/6 | | | 8/11 | | | Price |
|---|---|---|---|---|---|---|---|---|---|---|---|---|---|
| Stake | Win | 1/5 odds | 1/4 odds | Win | 1/5 odds | 1/4 odds | Win | 1/5 odds | 1/4 odds | Win | 1/5 odds | 1/4 odds | Stake |
| 5p | 0.07 | 0.05 | 0.05 | 0.08 | 0.05 | 0.05 | 0.08 | 0.05 | 0.05 | 0.08 | 0.05 | 0.05 | 5p |
| 10p | 0.15 | 0.11 | 0.11 | 0.16 | 0.11 | 0.11 | 0.16 | 0.11 | 0.11 | 0.17 | 0.11 | 0.11 | 10p |
| 20p | 0.31 | 0.22 | 0.22 | 0.32 | 0.22 | 0.23 | 0.33 | 0.22 | 0.23 | 0.34 | 0.22 | 0.23 | 20p |
| 50p | 0.78 | 0.55 | 0.57 | 0.80 | 0.56 | 0.57 | 0.83 | 0.56 | 0.58 | 0.86 | 0.57 | 0.59 | 50p |
| £1 | 1.57 | 1.11 | 1.14 | 1.61 | 1.12 | 1.15 | 1.66 | 1.13 | 1.16 | 1.72 | 1.14 | 1.18 | £1 |
| £2 | 3.14 | 2.22 | 2.28 | 3.23 | 2.24 | 2.30 | 3.33 | 2.26 | 2.33 | 3.45 | 2.29 | 2.36 | £2 |
| £3 | 4.71 | 3.34 | 3.42 | 4.84 | 3.36 | 3.46 | 5.00 | 3.40 | 4.08 | 5.18 | 3.43 | 3.54 | £3 |
| £4 | 6.28 | 4.45 | 4.57 | 6.46 | 4.49 | 4.61 | 6.66 | 4.53 | 4.66 | 6.90 | 4.58 | 4.72 | £4 |
| £5 | 7.85 | 5.57 | 6.40 | 8.07 | 5.61 | 5.76 | 8.33 | 5.66 | 5.83 | 8.63 | 5.72 | 5.90 | £5 |
| £6 | 9.42 | 6.68 | 6.85 | 9.69 | 6.73 | 6.92 | 10.00 | 6.80 | 7.00 | 10.36 | 6.87 | 7.09 | £6 |
| £7 | 11.00 | 7.80 | 8.00 | 11.30 | 7.86 | 8.07 | 11.66 | 7.93 | 8.16 | 12.09 | 8.01 | 8.27 | £7 |
| £8 | 12.57 | 8.91 | 9.14 | 12.92 | 8.98 | 9.23 | 13.13 | 9.06 | 9.33 | 13.81 | 9.16 | 9.45 | £8 |
| £9 | 14.14 | 10.02 | 10.28 | 14.53 | 10.10 | 10.38 | 15.00 | 10.20 | 10.50 | 15.54 | 10.30 | 10.63 | £9 |
| £10 | 15.71 | 11.14 | 11.42 | 16.15 | 11.23 | 11.53 | 16.66 | 11.33 | 11.66 | 17.27 | 11.45 | 11.81 | £10 |

| Price | 4/5 | | | 5/6 | | | 10/11 | | | 20/21 | | | Price |
|---|---|---|---|---|---|---|---|---|---|---|---|---|---|
| Stake | Win | 1/5 odds | 1/4 odds | Win | 1/5 odds | 1/4 odds | Win | 1/5 odds | 1/4 odds | Win | 1/5 odds | 1/4 odds | Stake |
| 5p | 0.09 | 0.05 | 0.06 | 0.09 | 0.05 | 0.06 | 0.09 | 0.05 | 0.06 | 0.09 | 0.05 | 0.06 | 5p |
| 10p | 0.18 | 0.11 | 0.12 | 0.18 | 0.11 | 0.12 | 0.19 | 0.11 | 0.12 | 0.19 | 0.11 | 0.12 | 10p |
| 20p | 0.36 | 0.23 | 0.24 | 0.36 | 0.23 | 0.24 | 0.38 | 0.23 | 0.24 | 0.39 | 0.23 | 0.24 | 20p |
| 50p | 0.90 | 0.58 | 0.60 | 0.91 | 0.58 | 0.60 | 0.95 | 0.59 | 0.61 | 0.97 | 0.59 | 0.61 | 50p |
| £1 | 1.80 | 1.16 | 1.20 | 1.83 | 1.16 | 1.20 | 1.90 | 1.18 | 1.22 | 1.95 | 1.19 | 1.23 | £1 |
| £2 | 3.60 | 2.32 | 2.40 | 3.66 | 2.33 | 2.41 | 3.81 | 2.36 | 2.45 | 3.90 | 2.38 | 2.47 | £2 |
| £3 | 5.40 | 3.48 | 3.60 | 5.50 | 3.50 | 3.62 | 5.72 | 3.54 | 3.68 | 5.85 | 3.57 | 3.71 | £3 |
| £4 | 7.20 | 4.64 | 4.80 | 7.33 | 4.66 | 4.83 | 7.63 | 4.72 | 4.90 | 7.80 | 4.76 | 4.95 | £4 |
| £5 | 9.00 | 5.80 | 6.00 | 9.16 | 5.83 | 6.04 | 9.54 | 5.90 | 6.13 | 9.76 | 5.95 | 6.19 | £5 |
| £6 | 10.80 | 6.96 | 7.20 | 11.00 | 7.00 | 7.25 | 11.45 | 7.09 | 7.36 | 11.71 | 7.14 | 7.42 | £6 |
| £7 | 12.60 | 8.12 | 8.40 | 12.83 | 8.16 | 8.45 | 13.36 | 8.27 | 8.59 | 13.66 | 8.33 | 8.66 | £7 |
| £8 | 14.40 | 9.28 | 9.60 | 14.66 | 9.33 | 9.66 | 15.27 | 9.45 | 9.81 | 15.61 | 9.52 | 9.90 | £8 |
| £9 | 16.20 | 10.44 | 10.80 | 16.50 | 10.49 | 10.87 | 17.18 | 10.63 | 11.04 | 17.57 | 10.71 | 11.14 | £9 |
| £10 | 18.00 | 11.60 | 12.00 | 18.33 | 11.66 | 12.08 | 19.09 | 11.81 | 12.27 | 19.52 | 11.90 | 12.38 | £10 |

| Price | Evens 1/1 | | | 21/20 | | | 11/10 | | | 6/5 | | | Price |
|---|---|---|---|---|---|---|---|---|---|---|---|---|---|
| Stake | Win | 1/5 odds | 1/4 odds | Win | 1/5 odds | 1/4 odds | Win | 1/5 odds | 1/4 odds | Win | 1/5 odds | 1/4 odds | Stake |
| 5p | 0.10 | 0.06 | 0.06 | 0.10 | 0.06 | 0.06 | 0.10 | 0.06 | 0.06 | 0.11 | 0.06 | 0.06 | 5p |
| 10p | 0.20 | 0.12 | 0.12 | 0.20 | 0.12 | 0.12 | 0.21 | 0.12 | 0.12 | 0.22 | 0.12 | 0.13 | 10p |
| 20p | 0.40 | 0.24 | 0.25 | 0.41 | 0.24 | 0.25 | 0.42 | 0.24 | 0.25 | 0.44 | 0.24 | 0.26 | 20p |
| 50p | 1.00 | 0.60 | 0.62 | 1.02 | 0.60 | 0.63 | 1.05 | 0.61 | 0.63 | 1.10 | 0.62 | 0.65 | 50p |
| £1 | 2.00 | 1.20 | 1.25 | 2.05 | 1.21 | 1.26 | 2.10 | 1.22 | 1.27 | 2.20 | 1.24 | 1.30 | £1 |
| £2 | 4.00 | 2.40 | 2.50 | 4.10 | 2.42 | 2.52 | 4.20 | 2.44 | 2.55 | 4.40 | 2.48 | 2.60 | £2 |
| £3 | 6.00 | 3.60 | 3.75 | 6.15 | 3.63 | 3.78 | 6.30 | 3.66 | 3.82 | 6.60 | 4.72 | 3.90 | £3 |
| £4 | 8.00 | 4.80 | 5.00 | 8.20 | 4.84 | 5.05 | 8.40 | 4.88 | 5.10 | 8.80 | 5.96 | 5.20 | £4 |
| £5 | 10.00 | 6.00 | 6.25 | 10.25 | 6.05 | 6.31 | 10.50 | 6.10 | 6.37 | 11.00 | 6.20 | 6.50 | £5 |
| £6 | 12.00 | 7.20 | 7.50 | 12.30 | 7.26 | 7.57 | 12.60 | 7.32 | 7.65 | 13.20 | 7.44 | 7.80 | £6 |
| £7 | 14.00 | 8.40 | 8.75 | 14.35 | 8.37 | 8.83 | 14.70 | 8.54 | 8.92 | 14.40 | 8.68 | 9.10 | £7 |
| £8 | 16.00 | 9.60 | 10.00 | 16.40 | 9.58 | 10.10 | 16.80 | 9.76 | 10.20 | 16.60 | 9.92 | 10.40 | £8 |
| £9 | 18.00 | 10.80 | 11.25 | 18.45 | 10.79 | 11.36 | 18.90 | 10.98 | 11.47 | 18.80 | 11.16 | 11.70 | £9 |
| £10 | 20.00 | 12.00 | 12.50 | 20.50 | 12.10 | 12.62 | 21.00 | 12.20 | 12.75 | 22.00 | 12.40 | 13.00 | £10 |

| Price | 5/4 | | | 11/8 | | | 6/4 | | | 13/8 | | | Price |
|---|---|---|---|---|---|---|---|---|---|---|---|---|---|
| Stake | Win | 1/5 odds | 1/4 odds | Win | 1/5 odds | 1/4 odds | Win | 1/5 odds | 1/4 odds | Win | 1/5 odds | 1/4 odds | Stake |
| 5p | 0.11 | 0.06 | 0.06 | 0.11 | 0.06 | 0.06 | 0.12 | 0.06 | 0.06 | 0.13 | 0.06 | 0.07 | 5p |
| 10p | 0.22 | 0.12 | 0.13 | 0.23 | 0.12 | 0.13 | 0.25 | 0.13 | 0.13 | 0.26 | 0.13 | 0.14 | 10p |
| 20p | 0.44 | 0.25 | 0.26 | 0.47 | 0.25 | 0.26 | 0.50 | 0.26 | 0.27 | 0.52 | 0.26 | 0.28 | 20p |
| 50p | 1.12 | 0.62 | 0.65 | 1.18 | 0.63 | 0.67 | 1.25 | 0.65 | 0.68 | 1.31 | 0.66 | 0.70 | 50p |
| £1 | 2.25 | 1.25 | 1.31 | 2.37 | 1.27 | 1.34 | 2.50 | 1.30 | 1.37 | 2.62 | 1.32 | 1.40 | £1 |
| £2 | 4.50 | 2.50 | 2.62 | 4.75 | 2.55 | 2.68 | 5.00 | 2.60 | 2.75 | 5.25 | 2.65 | 2.81 | £2 |
| £3 | 6.75 | 3.75 | 3.93 | 7.12 | 3.82 | 4.03 | 7.50 | 3.90 | 4.12 | 7.87 | 3.97 | 4.21 | £3 |
| £4 | 9.00 | 5.00 | 5.25 | 9.50 | 5.10 | 5.37 | 10.00 | 5.20 | 5.50 | 10.50 | 5.30 | 5.62 | £4 |
| £5 | 11.25 | 6.25 | 6.56 | 11.87 | 6.37 | 6.71 | 12.50 | 6.50 | 6.87 | 13.12 | 6.62 | 7.03 | £5 |
| £6 | 13.50 | 7.50 | 7.87 | 14.25 | 7.65 | 8.06 | 15.00 | 7.80 | 8.25 | 15.75 | 7.95 | 8.43 | £6 |
| £7 | 15.75 | 8.75 | 9.18 | 16.62 | 8.92 | 9.40 | 17.50 | 9.10 | 9.62 | 18.37 | 9.27 | 9.84 | £7 |
| £8 | 18.00 | 10.00 | 10.50 | 19.00 | 10.20 | 10.75 | 20.00 | 10.40 | 11.00 | 21.00 | 10.60 | 11.25 | £8 |
| £9 | 20.25 | 11.25 | 11.81 | 21.37 | 11.47 | 12.09 | 22.50 | 11.70 | 12.37 | 23.62 | 11.92 | 12.65 | £9 |
| £10 | 22.50 | 12.50 | 13.12 | 23.75 | 12.75 | 13.43 | 25.00 | 13.00 | 13.75 | 26.25 | 13.25 | 14.06 | £10 |

| Price | 7/4 | | | 15/8 | | | 2/1 | | | 85/40 | | | Price |
|---|---|---|---|---|---|---|---|---|---|---|---|---|---|
| Stake | Win | 1/5 odds | 1/4 odds | Win | 1/5 odds | 1/4 odds | Win | 1/5 odds | 1/4 odds | Win | 1/5 odds | 1/4 odds | Stake |
| 5p | 0.13 | 0.06 | 0.07 | 0.14 | 0.06 | 0.07 | 0.15 | 0.07 | 0.07 | 0.15 | 0.07 | 0.07 | 5p |
| 10p | 0.27 | 0.13 | 0.14 | 0.28 | 0.13 | 0.14 | 0.30 | 0.14 | 0.15 | 0.31 | 0.14 | 0.15 | 10p |
| 20p | 0.55 | 0.27 | 0.28 | 0.57 | 0.27 | 0.29 | 0.60 | 0.28 | 0.30 | 0.62 | 0.28 | 0.30 | 20p |
| 50p | 1.37 | 0.67 | 0.71 | 1.43 | 0.68 | 0.73 | 1.50 | 0.70 | 0.75 | 1.56 | 0.71 | 0.76 | 50p |
| £1 | 2.75 | 1.35 | 1.43 | 2.87 | 1.37 | 1.46 | 3.00 | 1.40 | 1.50 | 3.12 | 1.42 | 1.53 | £1 |
| £2 | 5.50 | 2.70 | 2.87 | 5.75 | 2.75 | 2.93 | 6.00 | 2.80 | 3.00 | 6.25 | 2.85 | 3.06 | £2 |
| £3 | 8.25 | 4.05 | 4.31 | 8.62 | 4.12 | 4.40 | 9.00 | 4.20 | 4.50 | 9.37 | 4.27 | 4.59 | £3 |
| £4 | 11.00 | 5.40 | 5.75 | 11.50 | 5.50 | 5.87 | 12.00 | 5.60 | 6.00 | 12.50 | 5.70 | 6.12 | £4 |
| £5 | 13.75 | 6.75 | 7.18 | 14.37 | 6.87 | 7.34 | 15.00 | 7.00 | 7.50 | 15.62 | 7.12 | 7.65 | £5 |
| £6 | 16.50 | 8.10 | 8.62 | 17.25 | 8.25 | 8.81 | 18.00 | 8.40 | 9.00 | 18.75 | 8.55 | 9.18 | £6 |
| £7 | 19.25 | 9.45 | 10.06 | 20.12 | 9.62 | 10.28 | 21.00 | 9.80 | 10.50 | 21.87 | 9.97 | 10.71 | £7 |
| £8 | 22.00 | 10.80 | 11.50 | 23.00 | 11.00 | 11.75 | 24.00 | 11.20 | 12.00 | 25.00 | 11.40 | 12.25 | £8 |
| £9 | 24.75 | 12.15 | 12.93 | 25.87 | 12.37 | 13.21 | 27.00 | 12.60 | 13.50 | 28.12 | 12.82 | 13.78 | £9 |
| £10 | 27.50 | 13.50 | 14.36 | 28.75 | 13.75 | 14.68 | 30.00 | 14.00 | 15.00 | 31.25 | 14.25 | 15.31 | £10 |

| Price | 9/4 | | | 5/2 | | | 11/4 | | | 3/1 | | | Price |
|---|---|---|---|---|---|---|---|---|---|---|---|---|---|
| Stake | Win | 1/5 odds | 1/4 odds | Win | 1/5 odds | 1/4 odds | Win | 1/5 odds | 1/4 odds | Win | 1/5 odds | 1/4 odds | Stake |
| 5p | 0.16 | 0.07 | 0.07 | 0.17 | 0.07 | 0.08 | 0.18 | 0.07 | 0.08 | 0.20 | 0.08 | 0.08 | 5p |
| 10p | 0.32 | 0.14 | 0.15 | 0.35 | 0.15 | 0.16 | 0.37 | 0.15 | 0.16 | 0.40 | 0.16 | 0.17 | 10p |
| 20p | 0.65 | 0.29 | 0.31 | 0.70 | 0.30 | 0.32 | 0.75 | 0.31 | 0.33 | 0.80 | 0.32 | 0.35 | 20p |
| 50p | 1.72 | 0.72 | 0.78 | 1.75 | 0.75 | 0.81 | 1.87 | 0.77 | 0.84 | 2.00 | 0.80 | 0.87 | 50p |
| £1 | 3.25 | 1.45 | 1.56 | 3.50 | 1.50 | 1.62 | 3.75 | 1.55 | 1.68 | 4.00 | 1.60 | 1.75 | £1 |
| £2 | 6.50 | 2.90 | 3.12 | 7.00 | 3.00 | 3.25 | 7.50 | 3.10 | 3.37 | 8.00 | 3.20 | 3.50 | £2 |
| £3 | 9.75 | 4.35 | 4.68 | 10.50 | 4.50 | 4.87 | 11.25 | 4.65 | 5.06 | 12.00 | 4.80 | 5.25 | £3 |
| £4 | 13.00 | 5.80 | 6.25 | 14.00 | 6.00 | 6.50 | 15.00 | 6.20 | 6.75 | 16.00 | 6.40 | 7.00 | £4 |
| £5 | 16.25 | 7.25 | 7.81 | 17.50 | 7.50 | 8.12 | 18.75 | 7.75 | 8.43 | 20.00 | 8.00 | 8.75 | £5 |
| £6 | 19.50 | 8.70 | 9.37 | 21.00 | 9.00 | 9.75 | 22.50 | 9.30 | 10.12 | 24.00 | 9.60 | 10.50 | £6 |
| £7 | 22.75 | 10.15 | 10.93 | 24.50 | 10.50 | 11.37 | 26.25 | 10.85 | 11.81 | 28.00 | 11.20 | 12.25 | £7 |
| £8 | 26.00 | 11.60 | 12.50 | 28.00 | 12.00 | 13.00 | 30.00 | 12.40 | 13.50 | 32.00 | 12.80 | 14.00 | £8 |
| £9 | 29.25 | 13.05 | 14.06 | 31.50 | 13.50 | 14.62 | 33.75 | 13.95 | 15.18 | 36.00 | 14.40 | 15.75 | £9 |
| £10 | 32.50 | 14.50 | 15.62 | 35.00 | 15.00 | 16.25 | 37.50 | 15.50 | 16.87 | 40.00 | 16.00 | 17.50 | £10 |

| Price | 100/30, 10/3 | | | 7/2 | | | 4/1 | | | 9/2 | | | Price |
|---|---|---|---|---|---|---|---|---|---|---|---|---|---|
| Stake | Win | 1/5 odds | 1/4 odds | Win | 1/5 odds | 1/4 odds | Win | 1/5 odds | 1/4 odds | Win | 1/5 odds | 1/4 odds | Stake |
| 5p | 0.21 | 0.08 | 0.09 | 0.22 | 0.08 | 0.09 | 0.25 | 0.09 | 0.10 | 0.27 | 0.09 | 0.10 | 5p |
| 10p | 0.43 | 0.16 | 0.18 | 0.45 | 0.17 | 0.18 | 0.50 | 0.18 | 0.20 | 0.55 | 0.19 | 0.21 | 10p |
| 20p | 0.86 | 0.33 | 0.36 | 0.90 | 0.34 | 0.37 | 1.00 | 0.36 | 0.40 | 1.10 | 0.38 | 0.42 | 20p |
| 50p | 2.16 | 0.83 | 0.91 | 2.25 | 0.85 | 0.93 | 2.50 | 0.90 | 1.00 | 2.75 | 0.95 | 1.06 | 50p |
| £1 | 4.33 | 1.66 | 1.83 | 4.50 | 1.70 | 1.87 | 5.00 | 1.80 | 2.00 | 5.50 | 1.90 | 2.12 | £1 |
| £2 | 8.66 | 3.33 | 3.66 | 9.00 | 3.40 | 3.75 | 10.00 | 3.60 | 4.00 | 11.00 | 3.80 | 4.25 | £2 |
| £3 | 13.00 | 5.00 | 5.50 | 13.50 | 5.10 | 5.62 | 15.00 | 5.40 | 6.00 | 16.50 | 5.70 | 6.37 | £3 |
| £4 | 17.33 | 6.66 | 7.33 | 18.00 | 6.80 | 7.50 | 20.00 | 7.20 | 8.00 | 22.00 | 7.60 | 8.50 | £4 |
| £5 | 21.66 | 8.33 | 9.16 | 22.50 | 8.50 | 9.37 | 25.00 | 9.00 | 10.00 | 27.50 | 9.50 | 10.62 | £5 |
| £6 | 26.00 | 10.00 | 11.00 | 27.00 | 10.20 | 11.25 | 30.00 | 10.80 | 12.00 | 33.00 | 11.40 | 12.75 | £6 |
| £7 | 30.33 | 11.66 | 12.83 | 31.50 | 11.90 | 13.12 | 35.00 | 12.60 | 14.00 | 38.50 | 13.30 | 14.87 | £7 |
| £8 | 34.66 | 13.33 | 14.66 | 36.00 | 13.60 | 15.00 | 40.00 | 14.40 | 16.00 | 44.00 | 15.20 | 17.00 | £8 |
| £9 | 39.00 | 15.00 | 16.50 | 40.50 | 15.30 | 16.87 | 45.00 | 16.20 | 18.00 | 49.50 | 17.10 | 19.12 | £9 |
| £10 | 43.33 | 16.66 | 18.33 | 45.00 | 17.00 | 18.75 | 50.00 | 18.00 | 20.00 | 55.00 | 19.00 | 21.25 | £10 |

| Price | 5/1 | | | 11/2 | | | 6/1 | | | 13/2 | | | Price |
|---|---|---|---|---|---|---|---|---|---|---|---|---|---|
| Stake | Win | 1/5 odds | 1/4 odds | Win | 1/5 odds | 1/4 odds | Win | 1/5 odds | 1/4 odds | Win | 1/5 odds | 1/4 odds | Stake |
| 5p | 0.30 | 0.10 | 0.11 | 0.32 | 0.10 | 0.11 | 0.35 | 0.11 | 0.12 | 0.37 | 0.11 | 0.13 | 5p |
| 10p | 0.60 | 0.20 | 0.22 | 0.65 | 0.21 | 0.23 | 0.70 | 0.22 | 0.25 | 0.75 | 0.23 | 0.26 | 10p |
| 20p | 1.20 | 0.40 | 0.45 | 1.30 | 0.42 | 0.47 | 1.40 | 0.44 | 0.50 | 1.50 | 0.46 | 0.53 | 20p |
| 50p | 3.00 | 1.00 | 1.12 | 3.25 | 1.05 | 1.18 | 3.50 | 1.10 | 1.25 | 3.75 | 1.15 | 1.31 | 50p |
| £1 | 6.00 | 2.00 | 2.25 | 6.50 | 2.10 | 2.37 | 7.00 | 2.20 | 2.50 | 7.50 | 2.30 | 2.62 | £1 |
| £2 | 12.00 | 4.00 | 4.50 | 13.00 | 4.20 | 4.75 | 14.00 | 4.40 | 5.00 | 15.00 | 4.60 | 5.25 | £2 |
| £3 | 18.00 | 6.00 | 6.75 | 19.50 | 6.30 | 7.12 | 21.00 | 6.60 | 7.50 | 22.50 | 6.90 | 7.87 | £3 |
| £4 | 24.00 | 8.00 | 9.00 | 26.00 | 8.40 | 9.50 | 28.00 | 8.80 | 10.00 | 30.00 | 9.20 | 10.50 | £4 |
| £5 | 30.00 | 10.00 | 11.25 | 32.50 | 10.50 | 11.87 | 35.00 | 11.00 | 12.50 | 37.50 | 11.50 | 13.12 | £5 |
| £6 | 36.00 | 12.00 | 13.50 | 39.00 | 12.60 | 14.25 | 42.00 | 13.20 | 15.00 | 45.00 | 13.80 | 15.75 | £6 |
| £7 | 42.00 | 14.00 | 15.75 | 45.50 | 14.70 | 16.62 | 49.00 | 15.40 | 17.50 | 52.50 | 16.10 | 18.37 | £7 |
| £8 | 48.00 | 16.00 | 18.00 | 52.00 | 16.80 | 19.00 | 56.00 | 17.60 | 20.00 | 60.00 | 18.40 | 21.00 | £8 |
| £9 | 54.00 | 18.00 | 20.25 | 58.50 | 18.90 | 21.37 | 63.00 | 19.80 | 22.50 | 67.50 | 20.70 | 23.62 | £9 |
| £10 | 60.00 | 20.00 | 22.50 | 65.00 | 21.00 | 23.75 | 70.00 | 22.00 | 25.00 | 75.00 | 23.00 | 26.25 | £10 |

| Price | 7/1 | | | 15/2 | | | 8/1 | | | 17/2 | | | Price |
|---|---|---|---|---|---|---|---|---|---|---|---|---|---|
| Stake | Win | 1/5 odds | 1/4 odds | Win | 1/5 odds | 1/4 odds | Win | 1/5 odds | 1/4 odds | Win | 1/5 odds | 1/4 odds | Stake |
| 5p | 0.40 | 0.12 | 0.13 | 0.42 | 0.12 | 0.14 | 0.45 | 0.13 | 0.15 | 0.47 | 0.13 | 0.15 | 5p |
| 10p | 0.80 | 0.24 | 0.27 | 0.85 | 0.25 | 0.28 | 0.90 | 0.26 | 0.30 | 0.95 | 0.27 | 0.31 | 10p |
| 20p | 1.60 | 0.48 | 0.55 | 1.70 | 0.50 | 0.57 | 1.80 | 0.52 | 0.60 | 1.90 | 0.54 | 0.62 | 20p |
| 50p | 4.00 | 1.20 | 1.37 | 4.25 | 1.25 | 1.43 | 4.50 | 1.30 | 1.50 | 4.75 | 1.35 | 1.56 | 50p |
| £1 | 8.00 | 2.40 | 2.75 | 8.50 | 2.50 | 2.87 | 9.00 | 2.60 | 3.00 | 9.50 | 2.70 | 3.12 | £1 |
| £2 | 16.00 | 4.80 | 5.50 | 17.00 | 5.00 | 5.75 | 18.00 | 5.20 | 6.00 | 19.00 | 5.40 | 6.25 | £2 |
| £3 | 24.00 | 7.20 | 8.25 | 25.50 | 7.50 | 8.62 | 27.00 | 7.80 | 9.00 | 28.50 | 8.10 | 9.37 | £3 |
| £4 | 32.00 | 9.60 | 11.00 | 34.00 | 10.00 | 11.50 | 36.00 | 10.40 | 12.00 | 38.00 | 10.80 | 12.50 | £4 |
| £5 | 40.00 | 12.00 | 13.75 | 42.50 | 12.50 | 14.37 | 45.00 | 13.00 | 15.00 | 47.50 | 13.50 | 15.62 | £5 |
| £6 | 48.00 | 14.40 | 16.50 | 51.00 | 15.00 | 17.25 | 54.00 | 15.60 | 18.00 | 57.00 | 16.20 | 18.75 | £6 |
| £7 | 56.00 | 16.80 | 19.25 | 59.50 | 17.50 | 20.12 | 63.00 | 18.20 | 21.00 | 66.50 | 18.90 | 21.87 | £7 |
| £8 | 64.00 | 19.20 | 22.00 | 68.00 | 20.00 | 23.00 | 72.00 | 20.80 | 24.00 | 76.00 | 21.60 | 25.00 | £8 |
| £9 | 72.00 | 21.60 | 24.75 | 75.50 | 22.50 | 25.87 | 81.00 | 23.40 | 27.00 | 85.50 | 24.30 | 28.12 | £9 |
| £10 | 80.00 | 24.00 | 27.50 | 85.00 | 25.00 | 28.75 | 90.00 | 26.00 | 30.00 | 95.00 | 27.00 | 31.25 | £10 |

| Price | 9/1 | | | 10/1 | | | 11/1 | | | 12/1 | | | Price |
|---|---|---|---|---|---|---|---|---|---|---|---|---|---|
| Stake | Win | 1/5 odds | 1/4 odds | Win | 1/5 odds | 1/4 odds | Win | 1/5 odds | 1/4 odds | Win | 1/5 odds | 1/4 odds | Stake |
| 5p | 0.50 | 0.14 | 0.16 | 0.55 | 0.15 | 0.17 | 0.60 | 0.16 | 0.18 | 0.65 | 0.17 | 0.20 | 5p |
| 10p | 1.00 | 0.28 | 0.32 | 1.10 | 0.30 | 0.35 | 1.20 | 0.32 | 0.37 | 1.30 | 0.34 | 0.40 | 10p |
| 20p | 2.00 | 0.56 | 0.65 | 2.20 | 0.60 | 0.70 | 2.40 | 0.64 | 0.75 | 2.60 | 0.68 | 0.80 | 20p |
| 50p | 5.00 | 1.40 | 1.62 | 5.50 | 1.50 | 1.75 | 6.00 | 1.60 | 1.87 | 6.50 | 1.70 | 2.00 | 50p |
| £1 | 10.00 | 2.80 | 3.25 | 11.00 | 3.00 | 3.50 | 12.00 | 3.20 | 3.75 | 13.00 | 3.40 | 4.00 | £1 |
| £2 | 20.00 | 5.60 | 6.50 | 22.00 | 6.00 | 7.00 | 24.00 | 6.40 | 7.50 | 26.00 | 6.80 | 8.00 | £2 |
| £3 | 30.00 | 8.40 | 9.75 | 33.00 | 9.00 | 10.50 | 36.00 | 9.60 | 11.25 | 39.00 | 10.20 | 12.00 | £3 |
| £4 | 40.00 | 11.20 | 13.00 | 44.00 | 12.00 | 14.00 | 48.00 | 12.80 | 15.00 | 52.00 | 13.60 | 16.00 | £4 |
| £5 | 50.00 | 14.00 | 16.25 | 55.00 | 15.00 | 17.50 | 60.00 | 16.00 | 18.75 | 65.00 | 17.00 | 20.00 | £5 |
| £6 | 60.00 | 16.80 | 19.50 | 66.00 | 18.00 | 21.00 | 72.00 | 19.20 | 22.50 | 78.00 | 20.40 | 24.00 | £6 |
| £7 | 70.00 | 19.60 | 22.75 | 77.00 | 21.00 | 24.50 | 84.00 | 22.40 | 26.25 | 91.00 | 23.80 | 28.00 | £7 |
| £8 | 80.00 | 22.40 | 26.00 | 88.00 | 24.00 | 28.00 | 96.00 | 25.60 | 30.00 | 104.00 | 27.20 | 32.00 | £8 |
| £9 | 90.00 | 25.20 | 29.25 | 99.00 | 27.00 | 31.50 | 108.00 | 28.80 | 33.75 | 117.00 | 30.60 | 36.00 | £9 |
| £10 | 100.00 | 28.00 | 32.50 | 110.00 | 30.00 | 35.00 | 120.00 | 32.00 | 37.50 | 130.00 | 34.00 | 40.00 | £10 |

| Price | 14/1 | | | 16/1 | | | 20/1 | | | 25/1 | | | 33/1 | | |
|---|---|---|---|---|---|---|---|---|---|---|---|---|---|---|---|
| Stake | Win | 1/5 odds | 1/4 odds | Win | 1/5 odds | 1/4 odds | Win | 1/5 odds | 1/4 odds | Win | 1/5 odds | 1/4 odds | Win | 1/5 odds | 1/4 odds |
| 5p | 0.75 | 0.16 | 0.22 | 0.85 | 0.21 | 0.25 | 1.05 | 0.25 | 0.30 | 1.30 | 0.30 | 0.36 | 1.70 | 0.39 | 0.46 |
| 10p | 1.50 | 0.38 | 0.45 | 1.70 | 0.42 | 0.50 | 2.10 | 0.50 | 0.60 | 2.60 | 0.60 | 0.72 | 3.40 | 0.76 | 0.92 |
| 20p | 3.00 | 0.76 | 0.90 | 3.40 | 0.84 | 1.00 | 4.20 | 1.00 | 1.20 | 5.20 | 1.20 | 1.45 | 6.80 | 1.52 | 1.85 |
| 50p | 7.50 | 1.90 | 2.25 | 8.50 | 2.10 | 2.50 | 10.50 | 2.50 | 3.00 | 13.00 | 3.00 | 3.62 | 17.00 | 3.80 | 4.62 |
| £1 | 15.00 | 3.80 | 4.50 | 17.00 | 4.20 | 5.00 | 21.00 | 5.00 | 6.00 | 26.00 | 6.00 | 7.25 | 34.00 | 7.60 | 9.25 |
| £2 | 30.00 | 7.60 | 9.00 | 34.00 | 8.40 | 10.00 | 42.00 | 10.00 | 12.00 | 52.00 | 12.00 | 14.50 | 68.00 | 15.20 | 18.50 |
| £3 | 45.00 | 11.40 | 13.50 | 51.00 | 12.60 | 15.00 | 63.00 | 15.00 | 18.00 | 65.00 | 18.00 | 21.75 | 102.00 | 22.80 | 27.75 |
| £4 | 60.00 | 15.20 | 18.00 | 68.00 | 16.80 | 20.00 | 84.00 | 20.00 | 24.00 | 104.00 | 24.00 | 29.00 | 136.00 | 30.40 | 37.00 |
| £5 | 75.00 | 19.00 | 22.50 | 85.00 | 21.00 | 25.00 | 105.00 | 25.00 | 30.00 | 130.00 | 30.00 | 36.25 | 170.00 | 38.00 | 46.25 |
| £6 | 90.00 | 22.80 | 27.00 | 102.00 | 25.20 | 30.00 | 126.00 | 30.00 | 36.00 | 156.00 | 36.00 | 43.50 | 204.00 | 45.60 | 55.50 |
| £7 | 105.00 | 26.60 | 31.50 | 119.00 | 29.40 | 35.00 | 147.00 | 35.00 | 42.00 | 182.00 | 42.00 | 50.75 | 238.00 | 53.20 | 64.75 |
| £8 | 120.00 | 30.40 | 36.00 | 136.00 | 33.60 | 40.00 | 168.00 | 40.00 | 48.00 | 208.00 | 48.00 | 58.00 | 272.00 | 60.80 | 74.00 |
| £9 | 135.00 | 34.20 | 40.50 | 153.00 | 37.80 | 45.00 | 189.00 | 45.00 | 54.00 | 234.00 | 54.00 | 65.25 | 306.00 | 68.40 | 83.25 |
| £10 | 150.00 | 38.00 | 45.00 | 170.00 | 42.00 | 50.00 | 210.00 | 50.00 | 60.00 | 260.00 | 60.00 | 72.50 | 340.00 | 76.00 | 92.50 |

| Price | 40/1 | | | 50/1 | | | 66/1 | | | 100/1 | | |
|---|---|---|---|---|---|---|---|---|---|---|---|---|
| Stake | Win | 1/5 odds | 1/4 odds | Win | 1/5 odds | 1/4 odds | Win | 1/5 odds | 1/4 odds | Win | 1/5 odds | 1/4 odds |
| 5p | 2.05 | 0.45 | 0.55 | 2.55 | 0.55 | 0.67 | 3.35 | 0.71 | 0.87 | 5.05 | 1.05 | 1.30 |
| 10p | 4.10 | 0.90 | 1.10 | 5.10 | 1.10 | 1.35 | 6.70 | 1.42 | 1.75 | 10.10 | 2.10 | 2.60 |
| 20p | 8.20 | 1.80 | 2.20 | 10.20 | 2.20 | 2.70 | 13.40 | 2.84 | 3.50 | 20.20 | 4.20 | 5.20 |
| 50p | 20.50 | 4.50 | 5.50 | 25.50 | 5.50 | 6.75 | 33.50 | 7.10 | 8.75 | 50.50 | 10.50 | 13.00 |
| £1 | 41.00 | 9.00 | 11.00 | 51.00 | 11.00 | 13.50 | 67.00 | 14.20 | 17.50 | 101.00 | 21.00 | 26.00 |
| £2 | 82.00 | 18.00 | 22.00 | 102.00 | 22.00 | 27.00 | 134.00 | 28.40 | 35.00 | 202.00 | 42.00 | 52.00 |
| £3 | 123.00 | 27.00 | 33.00 | 153.00 | 33.00 | 40.50 | 201.00 | 42.60 | 52.50 | 303.00 | 63.00 | 78.00 |
| £4 | 164.00 | 36.00 | 44.00 | 204.00 | 44.00 | 54.00 | 268.00 | 56.80 | 70.00 | 404.00 | 84.00 | 104.00 |
| £5 | 205.00 | 45.00 | 55.00 | 255.00 | 55.00 | 67.50 | 335.00 | 71.00 | 87.50 | 505.00 | 105.00 | 130.00 |
| £6 | 246.00 | 54.00 | 66.00 | 306.00 | 66.00 | 81.00 | 402.00 | 85.20 | 105.00 | 606.00 | 126.00 | 156.00 |
| £7 | 287.00 | 63.00 | 77.00 | 357.00 | 77.00 | 94.50 | 469.00 | 99.40 | 122.50 | 707.00 | 147.00 | 182.00 |
| £8 | 328.00 | 72.00 | 88.00 | 408.00 | 88.00 | 108.00 | 536.00 | 113.60 | 140.00 | 808.00 | 168.00 | 208.00 |
| £9 | 369.00 | 81.00 | 99.00 | 459.00 | 99.00 | 121.50 | 603.00 | 127.80 | 157.50 | 909.00 | 189.00 | 234.00 |
| £10 | 410.00 | 90.00 | 110.00 | 510.00 | 110.00 | 135.00 | 670.00 | 142.00 | 175.00 | 1010.00 | 210.00 | 260.00 |

# appendix 2

**abandoned racing** has been called off at that particular meeting

**accumulator** a bet on any number of selections, in different races, where the winnings on the first horse go onto the second, then onto the third, then onto the fourth and so on

**also-ran** a horse that lost

**awt** all weather fibre-sand track

**board price** the current price on offer for a horse

**bookies** betting shop or bookmakers

**boxed in** when a horse cannot overtake another because one or more horses block its path

**brought down** a horse that has fallen due to the actions of another horse

**bumper** a national hunt race

**burlington bertie** a price of 100/30

**carpet** a price of 3/1

**conditions race** a race where horses carry weight according to factors such as age, sex, whether they have won before or the type of race won

**connections** people related with a horse, such as the trainer and owner

**dead heat** where a race is a tie for either the winner or one of the placed horses

**double carpet** a price of 33/1

**draw** the position of a horse in the starting stalls

**dwelt** slow at the start

**evens** a price of 1/1

**faces** bookmakers' slang for punters with inside information about horses

**favourite** the horse with the lowest price

**fc** an abbreviation for forecast

**field** the runners in a race

**filly** a female horse up to 4-years-old

**first time out** a horse running in its first race

**form** a record of a horse's previous racing performance

**furlong** an eighth of a mile (201 metres)

**gelding** a castrated male horse

**the going** the condition of the racing surface

**going down** the horses are on their way to the start

**grand** £1,000

**green** a description of an inexperienced horse

**home stretch** the length of straight track before the finishing post

**IBAS** Independent Betting Arbitration Service, a British organization that settles disputes with bookmakers on the punter's behalf when the bookmaker is a member of the scheme

**inspection** due either to the weather or condition of the course; a decision will be made about whether or not racing can go ahead

**irons** stirrups

**juvenile** a 2-year-old horse

**lame** a horse that is having difficulty walking or is limping

**layers** bookmakers

**laying off** bookmakers' practice of reducing betting liability by betting with other bookmakers

**long shot** a horse with high odds

**maiden** a horse or rider that has not previously won a race

**match** a race where there are only two horses competing

**monkey** £500

**nap** the top tip of the day from a racing tipster

**novice** a horse in the early stages of its career after it has won its first race

**objection** a complaint from a jockey that, in his or her opinion, the rules of racing have been broken

**odds on** a price lower than evens

**off** the race has started

**outsider** a horse with little chance of winning

**pacer** a horse in harness racing which moves its legs on one side of its body in unison

**pari-mutuel** the prices quoted by the French tote

**pattern races in** Great Britain group 1, 2 and 3 races

**photo finish** a close race where the aid of a photograph is needed to determine the result

**plate** a shoe worn by a horse for racing

**pony** £25

**pulled up** a horse that drops out of the race after the off

**rag** a horse with little chance of winning (an outsider)

**rating** a measure of the performance of a horse on a scale of 0–140; 140 is the highest

**ready reckoner** a table showing returns for odds to aid the calculation of winnings

**rule 4** a deduction made from the prices due to the withdrawal of a horse from a race

**SP** an abbreviation for starting price

**scratching** a horse that is withdrawn from a race

**sidewheeler** a pacer in harness racing

**spread a plate** lose a horse shoe

**starter** the person responsible for starting the race

**steeplechase** a race over obstacles

**steward** a jockey club official who is responsible for checking that the rules of racing are followed

**stewards' enquiry** an inquiry into whether or not the rules of racing have been broken

**stud** where horses are bred

**stud book** a book that contains the pedigree of thoroughbred race horses

**system** a method of betting that is supposed to favour the player

**thoroughbred** a horse bred for racing that is registered in the *General Stud Book*

**tick-tac** hand signals used by bookmakers to communicate price changes

**tipster** a person who is employed by a newspaper to recommend horses that are likely to win

**tissue prices** early prices offered before a betting market has been formed

**trotter** a horse in harness racing that moves with a diagonal gait

**under orders** the race is about to start

**walkover** a race with only one runner. In order to be declared the winner, the horse must walk over the course. Where there are obstacles, the horse need not jump over them, but may walk around

**weigh-in** after each race the jockeys on the winning and placed horses must weigh in to confirm that they are carrying the same weight as at the start of the race

**yearling** a horse from 1 January to 31 December of the year following its birth

## Addresses

### Gamblers Anonymous organizations and the IBAS.

*Great Britain*
Gamblers Anonymous
National Service Office
PO Box 88
London SW10 OEU
Telephone 020 7384 3040
www.gamblersanonymous.org.uk/

*USA*
Gamblers Intergroup
PO Box 7
New York
New York 10116
Telephone 212 903 4400

*Australia*
Gamblers Anonymous
PO Box 142
Burwood NSW 1805
Telephone (02) 9564 1574
www.gamblersanonymous.org.au/

Independent Betting Arbitration Service (IBAS)
PO Box 4011
London E14 5BB

## Addresses of British race courses

Aintree Racecourse Co Ltd
Aintree
Liverpool L9 5AS
www.aintree.co.uk

Ascot Racecourse
Ascot
Berkshire SL5 7JN
www.ascot-authority.co.uk

The Western Meeting Club Racecourse Office
2 Whitletts Road
Ayr KA8 0JE
www.ayr-racecourse.co.uk

Bangor-on-Dee Races Ltd
The Racecourse
Wrexham LL13 0DA
www.bangordee.co.uk

The Bath Racecourse Co. Ltd
Lansdown
Bath BA1 9BU
www.comeracing.co.uk/bath.htm

The Beverley Race Co. Ltd
The Racecourse
York Road
Beverley
Yorks HU17 8QZ
www.goracing.co.uk

Brighton Racecourse Co Ltd
Freshfield Road
Brighton
East Sussex BN2 2XZ
www.brighton-racecourse.co.uk

Carlisle Racecourse Co. Ltd
Durdar Road
Carlisle
Cumbria CA2 4TS
www.carlisle-races.co.uk

Cartmel Steeplechases (Holker) Ltd
Cartmel
Nr Grange-over-Sands
Cumbria LA11 6QF
www.comeracing.co.uk/cartmel.htm

The Catterick Racecourse Co. Ltd
Catterick Bridge
Richmond
North Yorkshire DL10 7PE
www.catterickbridge.co.uk

Cheltenham Racecourse
Prestbury Park
Cheltenham
GL50 4SH
www.cheltenham.co.uk

Chepstow Racecourse plc
The Racecourse
Chepstow
Gwent NP6 5YH
www.chepstow-racecourse.co.uk

Chester Race Co. Ltd
The Racecourse
Cheshire CH1 2LY
www.chester-races.co.uk

Doncaster Racecourse
The Grandstand Leger Way
Doncaster
Yorks DN2 6BB
www.doncaster-racecourse.com

United Racecourses (Holdings)
The Grandstand
Epsom Downs
Surrey KT18 5LQ
www.epsomderby.co.uk

Devon + Exeter Steeplechases Ltd
The Racecourse
Halden
Nr Exeter
Devon EX2 4DE
www.comeracing.co.uk/exeter.htm

Fakenham Racecourse Ltd
The Racecourse
Fakenham
Norfolk NR21 7NY
www.comeracing.co.uk/fakenham.htm

Folkestone Racecourse plc
Westhanger
Hythe
Kent CT21 4HX
www.folkestone-racecourse.co.uk

Fontwell Park Steeplechase plc
Fontwell
Nr Arundel
West Sussex BN18 0SX
www.fontwellpark.co.uk

Goodwood Racecourse Ltd
Goodwood
Chichester
West Sussex PO18 0PS
www.goodwood.co.uk

The Hamilton Park Race Course Co. Ltd
Bothwell Road
Hamilton
Lanarkshire ML3 0DW
www.hamilton-park.co.uk

Haydock Park Racecourse Co. Ltd
Newton-le-Willows
Merseyside WA12 0HQ
www.haydock-park.com

Hereford Racecourse Co. Ltd
Shepherds Meadow
Eaton Bishop
Hereford HR2 9UA
www.comeracing.co.uk/hereford.htm

Hexham Steeplechase Co Ltd
The Ridings
Hexham
Northumberland NE46 4PF
www.hexham-racecourse.co.uk

Huntingdon Steeplechases Ltd
Brampton
Huntingdon
Cambridgeshire PE18 8NN
www.huntingdonracing.co.uk

Kelso Races Ltd Sale + Partners
18/20 Glendale Road
Wooler
Northumberland NE71 6DW
www.kelso-races.co.uk

United Racecourses (Holdings) Ltd
Kempton Park Racecourse
Sunbury-on-Thames TW16 5AQ
www.kempton.co.uk

Leicester Racecourse Co. Ltd
The Racecourse
Oadby
Leicester LE2 4AL
www.comeracing.co.uk/leiceste.htm

Lingfield Park (1991) Ltd
Racecourse Road
Lingfield
Surrey RH7 6PQ
www.lingfield-racecourse.co.uk

Ludlow Race Club Ltd
Shepherds Meadow
Eaton Bishop
Hereford HR2 9UA
www.ludlow-racecourse.co.uk

Market Rasen Racecourse Ltd
Legsby Road
Market Rasen
Lincs LN8 3EA
www.marketrasenraces.co.uk

Musselburgh Joint Racing Committee
Linkfield Road
Musselburgh
East Lothian EH21 7RG
www.musselburgh-racecourse.co.uk

Newbury Racecourse plc
The Racecourse
Newbury
Berkshire RG14 7NZ
www.newbury-racecourse.co.uk

High Gosforth Park Ltd
Newcastle Racecourse
High Gosforth Park
Newcastle upon Tyne NE3 5HP
www.comeracing.co.uk/newcastl.htm

Newmarket Racecourses Trust
Westfield House
Cambridge Road
Newmarket
Suffolk CB8 0TG
www.newmarketracecourses.co.uk

Newton Abbot Races Ltd
The Racecourse
Kingsteignton Road
Newton Abbot
Devon TQ12 3AF
www.naracecourse.co.uk

Nottingham Racecourse Co. Ltd
Colwick Park
Colwick Road
Nottingham NG2 4BE
www.nottinghamracecourse.co.uk

The Perth Hunt Perth Racecourse
Scone Palace Park
Perth PH2 6BB
www.perth-races.co.uk

Plumpton Racecourse Ltd
Plumpton
East Sussex BN7 3AL
www.plumptonracecourse.co.uk

Pontefract Park Race Co. Ltd Raceday only
tel/fax 01977 702210
33 Ropergate
Pontefract
West Yorkshire WF8 1LE
www.pontefract-races.co.uk

Redcar Racecourse Ltd
The Racecourse
Redcar
Cleveland TS10 2BY
www.www.redcarracing.co.uk

Ripon Race Co. Ltd
77 North Street
Ripon
North Yorkshire HG4 1DS
www.goracing.co.uk/detail.htm#ripon

The Bibury Club
Salisbury Racecourse
Netherhampton
Salisbury SP2 8PN
www.salisburyracecourse.co.uk

United Racecourse (Holdings) Ltd
The Racecourse
Esher
Surrey KT10 9AJ
www.sandown.co.uk

Sedgefield Steeplechase Co. (1927) Ltd
The Racecourse
Sedgefield
Stockton-on-Tees
Cleveland TS21 2HW
www.comeracing.co.uk/sedgefie.htm

RAM Racecourses Ltd
Rolleston
Southwell
Notts NG25 0TS
www.southwell-racecourse.co.uk

Stratford on Avon Racecourse Co. Ltd
Luddington Road
Stratford-upon-Avon CV37 9SE
www.stratfordracecourse.net

Taunton Racecourse Co. Ltd
Orchard Portman
Taunton
Somerset TA3 7BL
www.tauntonracecourse.co.uk

Thirsk Racecourse Ltd
Station Road
Thirsk
North Yorkshire YO7 1QL
www.goracing.co.uk/detail.htm#thirsk

Towcester Racecourse Co. Ltd
Easton Neston
Towcester
Northants NN12 7HS
www.towcester-racecourse.co.uk

Uttoxeter Leisure and Development Co. Ltd
The Racecourse Wood Lane
Uttoxeter
Staffs ST14 8BD
www.uttoxeterracecourse.co.uk

Warwick Racecourse
Hampton Street
Warwick CV34 6HN
www.warwickracecourse.co.uk

Wetherby Steeplechase Committee Ltd
The Racecourse York Road
Wetherby
North Yorkshire LS22 5EJ
www.wetherbyracing.co.uk

Wincanton Races Co. Ltd
The Racecourse
Wincanton
Somerset BA9 8BJ
www.wincantonracecourse.co.uk

Windsor Racing Ltd
The Racecourse
Windsor
Berkshire SL4 5JJ
www.windsorracing.co.uk

Dunstall Park Centre Ltd
Gorsebrook Road
Wolverhampton WV6 0PE
www.wolverhampton-racecourse.co.uk

Worcester Racecourse
Grandstand Road
Pitchcroft
Worcester WR1 3EJ
Website: www.worcester-racecourse.co.uk

Great Yarmouth Racecourse
Jellicoe Road
Great Yarmouth
Norfolk NR30 4AU
www.comeracing.co.uk/yarmouth.htm

York Race Committee
The Racecourse
York
Yorkshire YO23 1EX
www.yorkracecourse.co.uk

## Other useful addresses

*Great Britain*
The British Horseracing Board
42 Portman Square
London W1 6EN
Telephone 020 7396 0011
Fax 020 7935 0131
Email info@bbb.co.uk
www.bnb.co.uk

*Ireland*
Horse Racing Ireland
The Curragh
Co. Kildare
Ireland
Telephone 045 445645
Fax 045 445646
Email info@horseracingireland.ie
www.iha.ie

*USA*
Thoroughbred Racing Associations of North America
420 Fair Hills Drive
Suite 1
Elkton
MD
Zip 21921-2573
Telephone (410) 392 9200
Fax (410) 398 1366
Email info@tra-online.com
www.tra-online.com

United States Trotting Associations
750 Michigan Avenue
Columbus
OH 43215
Telephone (614) 224 2291
Fax (614) 228 1385
Email stats@ustrotting.com
www.ustrotting.com

## Website

How to Win
The website of Belinda Levez
www.clik.to/howtowin

# index